Politics Beyond Left and Right
A Guide for Creating a More Unified Nation

David A. Ellison

Laura,

To a more perfect Union!

David A. Ellison

*To the Founders of this great country and those
who still want to create a more perfect Union*

Contents

Introduction

"Clowns to the left of me,
Jokers to the right, here I am,
Stuck in the middle with you."

The lyrics from Stealers Wheel's famous song seem a fitting and appropriate way to describe how many, if not most, Americans feel about the current state of the political climate. Because the Democrats (Left) and Republicans (Right) in Washington, DC can hardly agree on anything, our country seems to be led by clowns and jokers, rather than elected officials who, in the interest of their constituents and the nation as a whole, should be preserving, protecting, and defending the Constitution of the United States of America.

Politically, this leaves most Americans feeling, as Stealers Wheel puts it, "stuck in the middle." I refer to those of us in the middle as Centrists, a term you may have heard, but one not often clearly and concisely defined. Simply, Centrists like some of the ideas from the Democratic side of the aisle and some from the Republican side. Centrists are not wishy-washy in their beliefs. We believe in a federal government that is smaller and more fiscally responsible than what Democrats prefer, but more socially accepting than what Republicans prefer.

Unfortunately, the Democrats on the far Left and the Republicans on the far Right—both with their own ideological views—hold their respective parties hostage, so it is difficult to get consensus and little gets done. I would like to think that a simple answer to our political woes would be the creation of a Centrist Party, but with the two main parties being so well-funded and strong, I don't believe a viable new party will emerge anytime soon. In the meantime, I will share with you what I perceive to be some of the views of those of us "stuck in the middle." I will attempt to accomplish this in the form of a pamphlet rather than a book, because pamphlets are smaller and most people don't have time for, or interest in, a long read. Pamphlets—smaller and less formal versions of a book—have played an important role in our nation's history. Given there was no radio or television in the 1700s, their distribution was the medium through which political sparring often took place. In our busy world, I believe it is time for pamphlets to make a comeback.

This pamphlet will cover a variety of subjects. I do not speak for all Centrists, so even if you consider yourself one, this does not necessarily mean you will agree with all my ideas. I am not so presumptuous to assume that I have all the answers to our nation's problems. But unlike our politicians, I like to hear constructive criticism and look forward to hearing from those of you with better solutions for improving our country.

Oddly, some people claim they have no interest in politics. I beg to differ, because when you think about it, politics affects every aspect of our lives. If you care about the type and cost of your healthcare; the cost of food, heating, electricity, clothing, automobiles, housing, insurance, entertainment, and vacations; the quality and cost of your children's education; or the ability to save for retirement, you care about politics, because it is our elected officials that determine how much of our hard-earned dollars we can keep. When you add up what you pay in income taxes, Social Security taxes, Medicare taxes, property taxes, and sales taxes, I bet it's a pretty large sum. Since our elected officials determine how they spend the money they take from us through taxation, I am sure you hope they aren't wasting your money.

According to Neil Boortz, former host of a syndicated radio talk show and author of *Somebody's Gotta Say It*, people who claim they are not interested in politics are making an "affirmation that [they are] not interested in the actions of people who control [their] bank account, [their] personal freedom, and [their] very life."[1] I am sure you care a great deal about yourself and your money, so whether you realize it or not, you are already interested in politics by default.

Understanding what is going on politically is critically important for the role you need to play in our political system. Yes, you have a role; we all have a role. Our role is to vote out elected officials who are not adhering to the Constitution and serving the public's best interest, and vote in people who will.

Getting back to your hard-earned money. Because everyone cares about their money, Mr. Boortz has gone so far as to propose that every time a congressman or senator co-sponsors a spending bill, he or she would be obligated to sign the following addendum: "I, _____, in sponsoring/co-sponsoring this bill, do hereby affirm that I believe it is more important that the United States federal government seize the money appropriated herein from the taxpayers to fund this bill, than to allow taxpayers who actually earned this money to retain it for their own needs."[2]

So far, and not surprisingly, Mr. Boortz's proposal has gone on deaf ears.

We live in the greatest country in the world, but unless we want to become the first generation to leave our children an America in worse shape than the one we were born into, we need good, civil communication and compromise between the Left and Right. It is my hope that this pamphlet can play a role in taking our nation in a more unifying and fiscally responsible direction.

Chapter 1
Always Remember Why
Our Ancestors Came to America

In order to get the most out of this pamphlet and effectively perform your political role of being an informed voter, I believe it is important for you to reflect back, put yourself in your ancestors' shoes, and develop a deep understanding as to why they came to America. Sadly, some of our ancestors were forced to come to America as slaves, but most chose to come to this great country because they felt they had a better opportunity to create the life they wanted for themselves and their families here than in their homeland.

Many of our ancestors were trying to leave a country where they were not free to own property and profit from the land, where hard work was not rewarded, and where economic and personal success were not readily attainable. Many wanted to leave a country where they were not allowed their own freedom of expression or thought—because of tyrannical governments. Many others wanted to leave a country where they were not allowed to worship as they saw fit.

Our ancestors came to America seeking freedom. They wanted to live, work, and worship the way they chose, and to escape large bureaucratic governments. They wanted the opportunity to create the life of their dreams, although there were no guarantees, as well as the opportunity for self-actualization through hard work. The countries many of our ancestors left had governments that were run only by a select few with no power held by *We the People*. They did not have a representative form of government with limited powers; often times these governments were all-powerful and left individuals with little or no opportunity to create their own economic success. Some governments owned the land and businesses, so all but a few people were dependent on the government for food, income, healthcare, and shelter. If your ancestors never came to America, can you imagine what your life would be like today?

As Americans, we want freedom and choices. We don't want a federal government that is so large that it dictates what we think and are allowed to do. We want a federal government that represents our interests and provides us with the services the U.S. Constitution dictates and a "safety net" for those unable to provide for themselves. And yes, we are willing to pay taxes to receive those benefits.

Arthur Brooks says in his book *The Road to Freedom* that the path our ancestors were on was the Free Enterprise System, which he describes as a "system of values and laws that respect private property and limits government, encourages competition and industry, celebrates achievement based on merit, and creates individual opportunity."[3] Dr. Brooks also states: "A system without opportunity, where merit was not rewarded, was what [our ancestors] were escaping *from* in Europe."[4]

Remembering why your ancestors came to America while you read this pamphlet will put you in the right frame of mind to get the most out of it, as it will reinforce all the benefits and freedoms we have as citizens of our great country, and underscore why their loss would be catastrophic. Given all the talk about income inequality, some of you may question whether economic success is still achievable by the masses. Happily, the research shows it is—if a Centrist approach is adopted.

Chapter 2
Political Parties Are Not Good vs. Evil

Democrats vs. Republicans. Left vs. Right. Liberals/Progressives vs. Conservatives. Call the two sides whatever you would like, just don't classify one as good and one as evil. As Yuval Levin points out in *The Great Debate: Edmund Burke, Thomas Paine, and the Birth of Right and Left*, each side is "passionately advancing its understanding of the common good."[5] If everyone kept that in mind, maybe there would be more civility, more compromise, less gridlock, and better outcomes.

If we start with the premise that both sides of the aisle are made up of good people, is it so hard to believe that each side has some good ideas but neither has a lock on all of them? The main areas of disagreement between the two political parties center around: the size and role of government; how to address the financial impact of entitlement programs; the tax code; healthcare; abortion; gay rights; our national debt, which is over $19 trillion dollars and growing; and income inequality. These and other important issues including racism, education, and immigration will be addressed in this pamphlet.

For those of us in the middle, we tend to side with the Right on financial matters as we know that if the government spends more than the revenue (taxes) it brings in over a long period of time, it will eventually go broke. Regarding social issues, we tend to lean toward the Left. I believe this combination of being fiscally responsible and socially accepting is what our country's Founders had in mind when they wrote the Declaration of Independence and the Constitution. Fiscal issues and social issues are both important; however, in my opinion, fiscal issues have more importance. This is because unless our country is on firm financial footing, it will eventually crumble, and social issues, like everything else, will become irrelevant.

Although each political party has its own philosophies on how to make our country a better place, the extreme sides of each party show some ironies at times. For instance, don't you feel it is ironic that the far Right of the Republican Party claims to favor the type of small federal government with few regulations that our Founders designed, yet they want to put their nose into our private life? And don't you find it ironic that the far Left of the Democratic Party—a party that claims to be the friend of the middle class and believers in democracy and "majority rule"—has put in place "administrative agencies" headed by powerful, non-elected officials without constitutional authority, and in doing so created a much larger and more expensive federal government with more regulatory control than our Founders designed? I do.

As Michelle Caruso-Cabrera, a CNBC news correspondent, said in her book *You Know I'm Right*, "I want a government that stays out of my pocketbook and stays out of my private life."[6]

Well said, Michelle!

Chapter 3
We Need Better Dialogue

For the Democrats and Republicans to solve our nation's fiscal and social problems, there must be honest, open dialogue—not just with the opposing party but within each party. I find it appalling that an elected official needs to be fearful of expressing views that run counter to the senior members in his or her own party because those views may affect his/her being chosen to sit on or head a certain committee. Think this doesn't happen? It even happens locally. Recently, when out to dinner with some friends, one of the women shared her experience being a political delegate at her party's convention. She planned to vote for the candidate whom she thought was the most qualified. However, when the party leaders learned she was not going to vote for "their guy," they told her that if she didn't vote as instructed, she would never again be a delegate and she could forget about ever being nominated for political office.

I believe that if we didn't have career politicians and set term limits for senators and congressmen, as we do for the president, we would see less of this intimidation and as a result, better dialogue. Term limits will be discussed in more detail later in the pamphlet. In the meantime, remember that just because you may be a member of a political party, it doesn't mean you have to be in agreement with your party on all issues; sometimes the other party's views on a particular subject make more sense. And when you believe the other party's candidate would do a better job in office, vote for that person.

Just as our elected officials need to have better dialogue, so do *We the People* who disagree on political and social issues. If we weren't afraid of having serious discussions with family, friends, and acquaintances regarding issues affecting our world, then we would learn from one another. This would lead to a better understanding as to why others think the way they do—an understanding which, as a nation, would put us in a position to make more informed decisions, and help us become a less divided country. In his book *One Nation*, Ben Carson gives a good explanation of our problem with having meaningful dialogue: "Rather than asking those with whom we disagree to clearly state their case, we set up rules of political correctness that mandate that their perspective must be the same as ours. We then demonize those with whom we disagree and as a result fail to reach any consensus that might solve our problems. We need to simply ignore the 'barking' and act like mature adults who can tolerate hearing something about which we disagree and still remain civil and open-minded."[7]

I have to admit, in this polarized world that is easier said than done. But, it is something for which we all must strive. Dr. Carson's solution is quite good: "The best way not to be easily injured by others' speech is to step out of the center of the circle so everything is not about you. By thinking about others and looking at things from other people's perspectives, there is much less time to feel that someone is picking on you or your interests."[8]

Unfortunately, some elected officials and activists do not seem to want important conversations to take place in a civilized way because that could lead to *compromise*, which could then negatively affect their role, their perceived significance in society, and their wealth. They often feign hypersensitivity for their own personal gain and not for the good of society.

Do not fear discussing politics, religion, racism, and other subjects you might have been instructed not to talk about with others. Frank discussions are healthy as a lot can be learned if you listen carefully to others. Be respectful, but do not succumb to political correctness. Let your feelings be known no matter how sensitive the subject, but also get to know the other person's perspective so you both can then make informed decisions.

As a point of clarification: just because I quote Dr. Carson doesn't mean I agree with him on all issues. For instance, I do not agree with his belief that people have a choice in being heterosexual or homosexual. I believe you are born with a tendency of being one or the other, and I will address this issue at a later point in the pamphlet.

Chapter 4
Racism

Speaking of better dialogue, racism is an appropriate issue to discuss next, as race has always played a big role in politics. Abraham Lincoln ended slavery in spite of the objection of Southern Democrats. Because Lincoln was Republican, blacks favored Republicans for many years. However, today the majority of blacks vote Democratic. What happened? In *The Right Path*, Joe Scarborough explains how Barry Goldwater's vote against the 1964 Civil Rights Act changed the tide and still impacts politics to this day: "Goldwater's vote on civil rights carried a historic significance for Republican candidates not just in 1964 but also for the five decades that followed.... After Goldwater became the party's nominee, his opposition to LBJ's civil rights legislation helped contribute to a massive fallout of support from African Americans."[9]

Obviously, for the Republicans to get such a small percentage of the black vote, they must be doing something drastically wrong. Is it Republican beliefs and policies that keep the vast majority of blacks from voting for them, or is it the Republicans' lack of skill in explaining and selling the benefits of their policies? Probably a combination of both.

Before sharing my views on racism, you should probably know a little about my background, and how it influenced me. While growing up in Meriden, Connecticut, my parents brought my sister and me to the Methodist church in our city. It was there we met the Woods, a black family with whom we developed a beautiful friendship that continues to this day—close to fifty years. Both sets of parents were serious individuals who loved to talk about current events. My parents would occasionally go with Mr. and Mrs. Woods to the NAACP Legal Defense Fund conference in New York, and I was fortunate to join them one year. It was the '60s and, of course, racial tensions around the country were high, but it never had any impact on the relationship between our two families.

Both Mr. Woods, a physical therapist and an incredibly hard worker, and Mrs. Woods made sure their children knew the benefits of a good education and also made sure they worked very hard in school. In addition to stressing education, they also taught their children superb social skills and demonstrated the need for an outstanding work ethic. Five successful children are a testament to their fine parenting.

Even after my parents moved to Florida in 1976 at the conclusion of my freshman year of college, I would stop by Meriden to see Mr. and Mrs. Woods. They always treated me like I was one of their own kids, and I loved them for that. And Mr. Woods was certainly not shy about letting me know if I did something he didn't feel was appropriate; that's why I call him my "Connecticut dad." Always the educator, today Mr. Woods regularly sends me articles about current issues to make sure I am not turning too conservative. And one of his sons is not only one of my best friends, but also my doctor.

My views about race were primarily influenced by my parents, the Woods, playing sports with black friends, learning about the life and struggles of Dr. Martin Luther King, Jr., and reading *Black Like Me*, the true story of a white man who, under the care of a dermatologist, had his skin color temporarily changed in 1959 so he could pass for a black man and experience firsthand what blacks had to endure in a world full of racists. All these contributed to my basic, lifelong belief that, no matter what the color of the skin, people are basically the same. There are some important things that differentiate individuals but color is not one of them; these will be covered later in the pamphlet. Unfortunately, my view is not accepted by everyone, as there are still many who prejudge others based on their color. This has to stop if we are going to create a more unified nation.

Second, I do not believe that racism is something anyone is born with. To prove that, just go to any daycare facility and watch the young kids play. They don't care about color; they are just out for a good time with whomever strikes their fancy. Kids are wonderful that way and should be looked upon as experts in race relations. Racism is a learned behavior taught by adults.

Third, because of the positive relationships I have had with blacks, my head must have been in the sand because until the last several years, I had incorrectly assumed racism was no longer as prevalent. This has caused me to miss some of the things my friends of color have had to endure, such as having to explain to their children that there is a percentage of the population that will not like or trust them because of the color of their skin, and about how careful they need to be if stopped by the police, particularly since the police are more fearful of the public in general after all the shootings that have occurred across our country. Racism has been here all along to some degree, but with all the protests, violence, and shootings across the country, I haven't seen it this blatant since the '60s.

Fourth, racism goes both ways; there are white racists and black racists. Some of this comes from a fear for one's own safety, which, if you watch the news, you know at times it is justified. But some of it comes from just plain ignorance. I believe the *ignorance* part of the equation is due to children receiving inferior education at home and in school. This needs to end because a properly educated populace would lead us to a more peaceful, prosperous society.

Fifth, I believe that socio-economics plays more of a factor in prejudice than the color of one's skin. If you are educated, have an engaging personality, are respectful of others, and are fun to be around, good people do not care about the color of your skin. That said, we know that not all people are good.

Sixth, from what I can see, racial and ethnic leaders like Al Sharpton promote racism for their own personal gain. You should YouTube Johnathan Gentry's comments on August 14, 2014 about the Ferguson, Missouri riots and his August 15, 2014 interview on Fox News. He lambasts Mr. Sharpton and other activists for "only showing up when something happens with police or Caucasians so they can fan the flame of racial tensions, and not showing up for black on black shootings in Chicago and Oakland."[10] I believe people like Mr. Sharpton have set race relations back a long way and are part of the reason for the division in our country.

In his book *Wealth, Poverty and Politics*, Stanford University professor Thomas Sowell speaks about the problem of racial and ethnic leaders who, throughout world history, have stirred resentful emotions in the groups they were leading and cast blame on others for their "group's failure to share more fully in the economic benefits created by skills and knowledge that [were] not as prevalent in [their group's culture.]"[11] He was not talking in terms of blacks against whites, as many times it was whites from one region in the world against whites from another region. He was just making a point that these kinds of leaders are dangerous as well as unproductive when it comes to improving their group's status in society.

Why do these leaders do that? I believe it was and is because of self-preservation. When a group acquires the skills and behaviors needed for success, leaders fear that their role will no longer exist. How shortsighted! Had these leaders played it correctly, they could have led the charge for the development of the necessary skills and behaviors, and come out looking like heroes.

Mr. Sharpton is no Martin Luther King, Jr., who believed that people should be judged not by the color of their skin, but by the content of their character. Sadly, it does seem like our country has gotten away from Dr. King's message. I believe the Black Lives Matter movement started out with good, peaceful intentions but it quickly turned course when the more militant got involved. I don't believe Dr. King would have approved of this change-in-course Black Lives Matter has taken with its anti-cop campaign. Is some of the anger justified? Absolutely. But the militant approach to solving the problems in the inner cities is not the peaceful approach Dr. King would have used, and it certainly isn't helping race relations in this country.

Although the U.S. Justice Department has proven that Michael Brown from Ferguson, Missouri was not shot down while trying to surrender, the anti-cop campaign continues in many cities across the United States. This is uncalled for, even though there have undoubtedly been incidents where police have used excessive force and killed unarmed people—but those killed weren't all black. Bad police officers are not the norm; the facts don't bear it out.

Heather Mac Donald from the Manhattan Institute gave a speech entitled "The Danger of the 'Black Lives Matter' Movement" on April 27, 2016 at Hillsdale College. I will share with you parts of the summary of her speech that was in the April edition of *Imprimis*, a publication of Hillsdale College. She started by talking about how police have an "obligation to treat everyone with courtesy and respect, and act within the confines of the law. [That] too often, officers develop a hardened, obnoxious attitude. That being stopped when you are innocent of any wrongdoing is infuriating, humiliating, and sometimes terrifying.

[That] given the history of racism in this country and the complicity of the police in that history, police shootings of black men are particularly and understandably fraught."[12] However, she also stated that the far larger problem is black-on-black crime, which is exactly the same message Johnathan Gentry was delivering on YouTube, and the reason we need better schools, particularly in the inner cities. I believe a better educated youth will have the marketable skills to get a good job and not turn to a life of crime.

Yes, we need police officers who are well-trained and treat everyone equally. And it would help if there were a way to test each officer candidate's level of racial prejudice. By the same token, we have to understand the stress officers have by continually putting themselves in harm's way, and see that it is not always easy for them to determine who is a friend or foe. Police officers working in inner-cities across the United States have a thankless job. While trying to protect the public, officers not only face physical danger, but sometimes harassment from bystanders, some of whom take cell phone videos that do not always show what precipitated an officer's reaction to a situation.

Below are some statistics Ms. Mac Donald shared in her speech:[13]

1. Every year, approximately 6,000 blacks are murdered. This is a number greater than white and Hispanic homicide victims combined, even though blacks are only 13 percent of the national population. The vast majority of these blacks were killed by other blacks.

2. Blacks of all ages commit homicide at eight times the rate of whites and Hispanics combined, and the astronomical black death-by-homicide rate is a function of the black crime rate.

3. The nation's police killed 987 civilians in 2015, according to a database compiled by the *Washington Post*. Whites were 50 percent—or 493—of those victims, and blacks were 26 percent—or 258.

4. Twelve percent of all white and Hispanic homicide victims are killed by police officers, compared to four percent of all black homicide victims.

5. Crime rates across the country were much higher 20 years ago. In New York City in 1990, there were 2,245 homicides. In 2014 there were 333—a decrease of 85 percent.

Ms. Mac Donald attributes much of the drop in New York's crime rate to a goal established by the NYPD in 1994 to prevent crime rather than just respond to it. To meet this goal, the NYPD gathered and analyzed crime data looking for patterns, then developed tactics based on those patterns. Commanders were held accountable for crime in their jurisdictions, and a sense of urgency in fighting crime was established. She states that this strategy led to local businesses setting up shop in formerly drug-infested areas, and that even senior citizens and children started to feel safe shopping and playing there. However, she is concerned that the "falsehoods of the Black Lives Matter movement" will put all this in jeopardy.[14]

Although I quoted some alarming statistics regarding black crime, I do not believe for one minute that this is a reflection on the black race as a whole. I believe it is a reflection of a socioeconomic problem resulting from a "failed system" that makes it difficult for some, both black and white, to elevate themselves in this society.

Children need to learn that the keys to economic success and a better quality of life are getting an excellent education, developing superb social skills, and having an outstanding work ethic. Obviously, there are no guarantees these three things will bring everyone the success they desire, but they are the first things needed for developing the marketable skills necessary to elevate oneself in this society. Unfortunately, there are many children who face daunting obstacles on their road to economic success. One obstacle could be a parent who may have lost faith in the ability to get ahead in the world, and chooses to pass this negative attitude down to future generations rather than the positive one stated above. When this is the case, direction from a good role model outside the home would be invaluable to a child. This could come from an adult relative or friend, local businessperson, a member of the clergy, or a teacher.

Another obstacle could be the people a child associates with, particularly ones in their own neighborhood who are not a good influence. Children living in poor areas are often exposed to criminals and drug addicts, and often looked down upon and sometimes tormented by these people if they behave properly and are serious about doing well in school.

Unfortunately, many children face what I believe is a preventable obstacle: no access to a high-quality education. This needs to change. Sadly, even if all schools in the country were immediately elevated to a high-quality, it would not immediately change the condition of currently poor neighborhoods, but such an approach is the best long-term solution. With this in mind, it is time to discuss education in detail as it is one of the keys—and maybe *the* key—to reducing racism and crime.

Chapter 5
Education

This could possibly be the most important chapter in the pamphlet, as I and many others believe that an educated populace is the answer to many of our country's problems. Since you are most certainly interested in enjoying the benefits of a more peaceful, prosperous nation, you should note that to have these benefits, you need an educated society.

In his book *I Got Schooled*, movie director M. Night Shyamalan shared a quote from a book Frenchmen Alexis de Tocqueville wrote in the 1830s, *Democracy in America*, that explains the importance of an educated society—a topic that is as relevant today as it was when it was written: "I do not think that the system of self-interest as it is professed in America is in all its parts self-evident, but it contains a great number of truths so evident that men, if they are only educated, cannot fail to see them. Educate, then, at any rate, for the age of implicit self-sacrifice and instinctive virtues is already flitting far away from us, and the time is fast approaching when freedom, public peace, and social order itself will not be able to exist without education."[15] An excellent education, I would add.

With what has been going on in this country, it is almost as if Mr. Tocqueville is speaking directly to us today. We need to heed his advice before it is too late. Rational people all agree that it is critically important that every child in America have access to a high-quality education. Unfortunately, some statistics show the United States is falling behind other countries when it comes to educating our youth. What those statistics don't reveal is that the children from more affluent families are doing much better than those from the poorer neighborhoods and are just as smart as the children from other countries. We just need to fix the system—particularly in our poorer neighborhoods—because until we do, we will not be the peaceful, prosperous nation we could be.

One of the main problems with our current educational system is that there is no incentive for teachers to improve their performance. And because of tenure, there is little or no penalty for a teacher with a subpar performance. This must change if all our youth are going to have an equal opportunity of getting a high-quality education.

The answer to a better educational system is not about the government spending more money, hiring more teachers, or designing a new curriculum; it is about allowing parents to have the freedom to choose how their money is spent to educate their children. For those of you with children in a public school, you may be thinking that you aren't paying anything because public schools are free. Think again. The local taxes you pay allow your children to attend public school. So, make no mistake, you are paying for your children's education. The question is, is there a way for your children to get a better education for the same amount of money that you are currently paying? Yes, and it is called *school choice*.

Michelle Caruso-Cabrera states in her book *You Know I'm Right*, "Choice has made our university system the best in the world. The university system is based on competition and succeeds because attendance isn't determined by zip codes. We are the envy of the world when it comes to higher education, and yet we offer some of the weakest programs in elementary and high schools."[16]

Our country was built on the belief that a free enterprise system, one that encourages competition, will assure the best results for *We the People*. With competition, products and services are improved and price comes down. Yet, we don't see competition in our educational system. Since you have no choice but to pay for your local public school system—even if you pay for your children to attend private school—the government is in effect acting as a monopoly, which is an organization that sells a product or service only they can offer and has been determined to be harmful to the public and illegal. So how do we move from a monopolistic system to one based on choice and competition? A properly run *voucher system*.

A voucher system allows parents to have some of the money they pay in local taxes sent directly to their school of choice for their children. However, for a voucher system to be fair for all—no matter what one's financial status—there must be some strict parameters in place.

So how do you make the voucher system fair? Ms. Caruso-Cabrera writes, "In an ideal voucher system as envisioned by the Milton Friedman Foundation, participating schools must follow only a few rules. If a school has more applicants than spaces, they must hold a random lottery to fill the slots. This ensures they don't cherry-pick the students with the best grades or disallow students with poor academic records. Participating schools must have a uniform, simple application process. The minute there are 'extra' requirements such as parent interviews, poor and working parents are at a disadvantage. And finally, they must meet certain safety standards and financial standards."[17]

It is my belief that all children need to master reading, math, the Declaration of Independence, and the U.S. Constitution. With excellent reading and math skills, you can excel in all other courses. With an excellent understanding of the Declaration of Independence and the U.S. Constitution, you gain a deeper appreciation of why and how our nation was formed, as well as a better awareness of what you should and should not expect from our federal government. This leads to a greater sense of pride in being part of this great nation, and makes you want to become a more productive member of society.

I also believe that children need fun, practical science classes to pique their interest. From my experience, most science teachers do not make their classes exciting or stimulate a student's imagination. This needs to change because we need more people gravitating to careers in science and engineering. Of course, students also need a good background in history.

M. Night Shyamalan strongly believes that if "choice" is going to be part of our educational system, then there should be "no bad choices," and that every school in America should be able to provide its students a high-quality education. In his quest to close "America's education gap," defined as the difference in the quality of education the students in top quartile schools receive in relation to those in the bottom quartile schools, Mr. Shyamalan researched what the best schools across the country are doing and came up with his Five Keys to providing a top-notch school and eliminating this gap. And he found that there was a significant drop off if not *all* Five Keys were present in a school. Below is a summary of his Keys, but I suggest getting a copy of his book *I Got Schooled* for a more detailed explanation.

First Key: No Roadblock Teachers[18]

Mr. Shyamalan's research shows that maybe the most important key to closing the achievement gap is increasing the odds that kids receive great—or, at least, 'good'—instruction for four years in a row by making sure they don't hit a roadblock (inferior) teacher along the way. Every school he visited that is closing the achievement gap regularly lets go of their lowest-performing teachers.

He believes inferior teachers are costing those subjected to bad teachers and our country a fortune. Because of this, schools need an accurate method of evaluating teacher performance and value. The method found to be the best is a combination of the review of data collected from teacher observations and videotape, student learning growth as measured by a student's actual progress in comparison to expected progress, and student surveys that ask the right questions, the ones that really get at what matters inside the classroom, not whether they like a teacher. With the elimination of tenure and the ability of a school to be able to decide who should no longer be teaching our children, we would be on the right path to a more consistent, better-quality educational system in this country.

Second Key: The Right Balance of Leadership[19]

School leadership is second only to classroom teaching as an influence on learning, according to Mr. Shyamalan, and his research showed the following:

1. The most successful teams work under the most successful bosses.
2. The boss' most important job isn't communicating strategy or even hiring and firing. It's teaching skills that persist. Motivating a team of subordinates isn't nearly as important as improving their skills that lead to increased productivity. Therefore, the most effective school principals are the ones who spend most of their time in the classroom observing and instructing teachers, and who have an operations manager to handle everything other than instruction.

3. The most effective school principals have, in closing the education gap, created a culture of high expectations in teachers and students, and provided students with a more consistent experience from year to year.

Third Key: Feedback[20]

In order to provide all children with a high-quality educational experience, Mr. Shyamalan learned that it was important to find out what was working and what was not working in one classroom, and then make sure that every classroom implemented what worked well and discarded what didn't. It became evident to him that to give meaningful feedback to teachers, it was necessary to collect data regarding the curriculum, teacher technique, and student progress. He found that the feedback had to be meticulous, frequent, mandatory, and that it had to be produced in a form that was usable because there was absolutely no evidence that collecting data had any effect until it was understandable to every teacher in a school.

Fourth Key: Smaller Schools[21]

With the principal having more of an instructional role than an administrative role, Mr. Shyamalan's research concluded that the principal would be more effective with a smaller school to oversee so he could spend an appropriate amount of time in each class. It also concluded that the effectiveness level of the principal drops off when the number of students in a school exceeds 600.

Mr. Shyamalan points out that despite a common belief that there are economies-of-scale in building larger schools, his research found that it is less expensive on a per student basis and a square foot basis to build a school that can accommodate fewer than 725 students than it is to build one for 1,600 to 2,500 students.

Fifth Key: More Time in School[22]

Mr. Shyamalan and many others believe that American schools are not as good as they could be because they still run on a nineteenth-century, "let's-get-the-kids-out-of-school-so-they-can-help-with-the-harvest schedule." Prior to the Civil War, Philadelphia's schools were open 250 days per year and New York's were open all year, other than a two-week break in August. That's a far cry from the 180 days we have today.

His research found that studies have been done showing children from lower-income families stayed *relatively even* with their upper-income classmates while school was in session, but fell behind dramatically every summer, with a widening gap every year thereafter. *Relatively even* in this context means that if there was a difference in aptitude, it didn't widen during the school year. One study showed it even shrunk during the school year, but the cumulative effect of summer vacations was just as damaging over the long-term. This proves that children have a much better chance of academic success if they have parents who understand and teach the value of a good education and make sure their children continually improve their reading and math skills while not in school.

Fortunately, Mr. Shyamalan found that more time in school can counteract the effects of growing up in a family where education is not a priority. He feels that adding the additional hours can be accomplished in a variety of ways, such as extending the school day to 4:30, occasionally adding Saturday classes, having a shorter summer break, or instituting a mandatory three to four weeks of summer school.

Some Personal Thoughts

In addition to how and what our children are being taught, one of the problems I see with our educational system is that too many students are pushed toward a typical four year high school and then a typical four year college when clearly that is not where their interests lie. One of the goals of education is to learn a marketable skill so you can earn a good living and create your own economic success. Some people are more interested in and have the aptitude for working with their hands and would benefit from learning a trade at a vocational school. These people should be encouraged to consider this alternate, worthwhile path. Tradesmen are always in demand, can earn a great living, and never have to worry about their job being outsourced to a foreign country.

Better educated children will become better educated adults, and when that happens we will become a more unified, peaceful, and prosperous nation. Implementing the Five Keys into our schools, allowing school choice with a voucher system, exposing children to the opportunities at vocational schools, and letting some amazing schools compete for our children sounds like a winning combination to me. Let's get started!

Chapter 6
The Declaration of Independence
& the U. S. Constitution

I believe it is critically important for all American citizens to have a good understanding of these two important documents. We citizens need a deep understanding of each, as well as a deep understanding of how the two are connected, so we can monitor whether our elected officials are following the principles of the Declaration of Independence and the laws that were established in the U.S. Constitution to carry out its mission. Without this understanding, *We the People* will not be in a position to know when the far Left or far Right is advocating something that is unconstitutional and counter to our Founders' wishes. And unconstitutional is against the law.

Centrists reject the extreme views of the far Right and Far Left that fuel hate and violence. We prefer to adhere to our founding principles, and believe that it is only proper to deviate from them after there is a Constitutional Amendment. Unless you understand the two documents, how are you going to know when you are being led astray?

Our Founders were willing to sacrifice everything in order to achieve the goals laid out in the Declaration of Independence, and there is no better proof than in the last sentence of this precious document: "And for the support of this Declaration, with firm reliance on the protection of divine Providence, we mutually pledge to each other our Lives, our Fortunes and our sacred Honor." Because of this, I firmly believe that every student studying in the United States should, during his or her high school years, be required to pass a course that is focused solely on the Declaration of Independence and the U.S. Constitution. Yes, these two documents are briefly discussed as part of a course in U.S. History, but this isn't good enough. I believe we must honor our Founders by studying to understand them.

For those of us who have already completed our formal schooling, it is not too late to continue with our education. Hillsdale College offers an excellent, free U.S. Constitution course online that I cannot recommend highly enough. Although the course is free, I do suggest purchasing *The Founders' Key*, a book written by Larry Arnn, the president of Hillsdale College. In the book, he clearly explains the connection between the Declaration and the Constitution, and upon completion you will find a new sense of patriotism and pride.

Some believe that the Declaration of Independence and the Constitution are not connected. That is strange to me given that Thomas Jefferson, primary author of the Declaration, and James Madison, primary author of the Constitution, were best of friends and political allies. And both individuals assisted George Mason in writing the Virginia Declaration of Rights and the Virginia Constitution. In *The Founders' Key*, Dr. Arnn writes: "There is significant overlap between the text of the Virginia Declaration and the Virginia Constitution, and both overlap significantly with the Declaration of Independence and the Constitution of the United States. So if the latter two documents are 'incompatible,' the Virginia Convention instituted this incompatibility in two documents that are as close as hand and glove. And then two of the people responsible, if one counts Jefferson as a collaborator, went on to write the Declaration of Independence and the Constitution of the United States, all while remaining the closest political friends. And they managed, somehow, to make those two documents incompatible as well? Modern scholars ask us to believe this."[23]

Abraham Lincoln also saw a deep connection between the Declaration and the Constitution. He is known to have referred to our two most important documents as "an apple of gold, [the Declaration], in a frame of silver, [the Constitution]."[24] I choose to believe Mr. Lincoln rather than some of the so-called scholars of today who claim there is no connection.

Knowing that some of you will not get around to taking a U.S. Constitution course, I want to take the rest of this chapter to address one of the areas where the Founders have run into some criticism over the years—namely how they dealt with the subject of slavery in the Constitution, given that they previously declared "all men are created equal," and why it took so long before the institution was legally eliminated.

I believe that the original Article I, Section 2 of the Constitution has often been misinterpreted when it comes to the issue of slavery. Although slavery is not specifically mentioned, it is implied when the

25

Founders explain the number of people each state will be allowed in the House of Representatives. The formula was "determined by adding to the whole Number of free Persons, including those bound to Service for a Term of Years, and excluding Indians not taxed, three fifths of all other Persons, [and that the] Number of Representatives shall not exceed one for every thirty Thousand, but each state shall have at Least one Representative." Therefore, in the calculation, slaves were considered to equal three fifths of a free person. Sadly, some people have interpreted this to mean that our Founders believed individual slaves should not be looked upon as a complete person. That is an incorrect interpretation.

The states in favor of slavery wanted slaves to be counted the same as a free person so they would be credited with a larger population, which would entitle them to more Representatives and influence in Congress. The states against slavery and looking to abolish it, of course, didn't want the "slave states" to have more influence than necessary, so they didn't want slaves to be counted as a person. The two sides battled back and forth and ended up compromising on *three fifths*. It would have been better for the slaves to have not been counted at all, because counting them probably prolonged the hideous institution of slavery.

To get a better understanding of why it took so long to eliminate slavery, *The Founder's Key* is very informative. In the meantime, below are a couple quotes from Dr. Arnn's book that show why it was, unfortunately, not practical to eliminate slavery immediately at the time the Constitution was written, and that attempting to do so might have prevented the forming of our Union.

From John Jay, the first Chief Justice of the Supreme Court and a proponent of abolition: "The great body of our people had been so long accustomed to the practice and conveniences of having slaves, that very few among them even doubted the propriety and rectitude of it. Then liberal and conscientious men began to draw the lawfulness of slavery into question. Their doctrines prevailed by almost insensible degrees. We have good reason to hope and believe that if the natural operations of truth are constantly watched and assisted, but not forced and precipitated, then abolition can be achieved. Many of the legislatures in different states are proprietors of slaves, and therefore a total and sudden stop to this species of oppression is not to be expected."[25]

From Abraham Lincoln: "The authors of the Declaration of Independence did not mean to assert the obvious untruth, that all were then actually enjoying that equality, nor yet, that they were about to confer it immediately upon them. In fact, they had no power to confer such a boon. They meant simply to declare the right, so that the enforcement of it might follow as fast as circumstances should permit. They meant to set up a standard maxim for free society, which should be familiar to all, and revered by all; constantly looked to, constantly labored for, and even though never perfectly attained, constantly approximated, and thereby constantly spreading and deepening its influence, and augmenting the happiness and value of life to all people of all colors everywhere."[26]

The Founders knew that they, along with everyone else, were not perfect individuals. They believed only God could be perfect. However, our Founders were undoubtedly geniuses, and the documents they created should be studied by all.

Chapter 7
God-Fearing & Disciplined

In addition to needing a better educated society, I also believe that having parents raise their children in God-fearing, disciplined homes would go a long way toward elevating our society and bringing us all closer together.

I am not advocating one religion over another, nor am I advocating that parents make out God to be some "scary dude." I am advocating for parents teaching their children that God loves everyone. I am advocating for parents teaching their children that God is available for them to talk to at all times and is someone to lean on, particularly at difficult times. I am advocating for parents teaching their children to be grateful for what they have. I am advocating for parents teaching the Golden Rule: "Do unto others as you would have them do unto you." I am advocating for a more accepting, peaceful society.

Notice I am not advocating for some government regulation to create this more peaceful society. We have more than enough government regulations in this country already.

Although a fan of God, I am not a fan of religious institutions and factions trying to influence American politics, laws, and our elected officials. We are a country founded upon limited government. Religious institutions and factions with their own agendas only get in the way of a more peaceful society. They should teach their parishioners about God's good works and their interpretation of how God wants people to behave and live life, and stay out of politics and government.

John Lennon in his song "Imagine" asks us what the world would be like with no religion. He did not question what it would be like without God. I didn't know John, but I imagine that he was quite spiritual and, like many of us, possibly troubled that religions have been the cause of so many wars around the world.

As can be seen in the Declaration of Independence, our country's Founding Fathers were also spiritual. God is referenced several times in this precious document, with the most notable coming in the following words:

"We hold these truths to be self-evident, that all men are created equal, that they are endowed by their Creator with certain unalienable Rights, that among these are Life, Liberty and the pursuit of Happiness."

Quick history lesson: In the above quote from the Declaration of Independence, please note that the Founders were not guaranteeing Happiness.

Chapter 8
What Should We Expect
from Our Federal Government?

In this better educated, kinder, more peaceful and prosperous society we all want to create, what is it, then, that we Americans should expect from our government?

We should only expect what the Declaration of Independence states we are entitled to and what is promised in our Constitution: a government designed to carry out the mission of the Declaration. From the Declaration, we should all expect the following:

1. To be treated equally.
2. The right to life, liberty, and the pursuit of happiness.
3. To have governments (federal, state, and local) that derive their just powers from the consent of the governed, and that whenever any form of government becomes destructive of these ends, it is the right of the people to alter or abolish it, and to institute a new government based on the original principles.

Based on what the Constitution allows Congress to do, we should only expect the following from our government:

1. To have a federal government with the power to lay and collect taxes, duties, imposts, and excises to pay the debts and provide for the common defense and general welfare of the United States, and that all duties, imposts and excises shall be uniform throughout the United States. (This is the general statement from Article 1, Section 8 that precedes the following enumerated powers of Congress that are relevant today.)
2. To borrow money on the credit of the United States.
3. To have clear regulations regarding commerce, naturalization, bankruptcy.
4. To have a form of money with laws to protect against counterfeiting.
5. To establish post offices and roads for delivery.

6. To give authors and inventors exclusive right to their respective writings and discoveries for a limited period of time.

7. To have a Supreme Court and courts of law that are subordinate to the Supreme Court.

8. To define and punish piracies and felonies committed at sea.

9. To declare war.

10. To form a regulated Army and Navy.

11. To make rules for the government.

12. To suppress insurrections and repel invasions.

13. To make all laws that are necessary for carrying out the powers listed above and all other powers vested by the Constitution in the government of the United States, or in any department or officer thereof.

All of that is pretty straightforward except number one above, the general statement from Article 1, Section 8, particularly the words "providing for the general welfare of the United States." This clause has caused a lot of debate and chaos over the years. To understand the clause, two resources must be studied. One is the 1828 *American Dictionary of the English Language* by Noah Webster. The other is *The Federalist*, more commonly known as *The Federalist Papers*, a collection of essays promoting the ratification of the Constitution. Its writers were Alexander Hamilton, John Jay, and James Madison, the last of whom was the chief architect of our Constitution.

One must remember that the language used when our country was being formed is quite different from what it is today. Because of that, the definition of a word used back then is often different from today's definition. This can be confusing, so in order to understand what the Constitution is saying, we need to understand the older definitions. To understand the meaning of "general welfare," let's first look at the meaning of each word individually. When used as an adjective, "general" is defined in Webster's 1828 dictionary as:

1. Properly, relating to a whole genus or kind; and hence, relating to a whole class or order.

2. Public; common; relating to or comprehending the whole community; as the general interest or safety of a nation.

3. Having a relation to all; common to the whole.

"Welfare" is a noun that is defined in Webster's 1828 Dictionary as:

1. Exemption from misfortune, sickness, calamity or evil; the enjoyment of health and the common blessings of life; prosperity; happiness; applied to persons.

2. Exemption from any unusual evil or calamity; the enjoyment of peace and prosperity, or the ordinary blessings of society and civil government; applied to states.

When you look at the above definitions, it is obvious that the Founders intended "general welfare" to mean the enjoyment of the ordinary blessings of society and civil government—specifically those enumerated after the "general welfare clause"—by the whole population of the United States, and not merely specific subsections of it. Keep in mind that "individual rights" weren't addressed by our Founders until the Amendments were added to the Constitution at a later date, so "general welfare" had and has nothing to do with individuals per se, but rather society as a whole.

Unfortunately, what has happened over the past 100 years or so is that many of our elected officials have expanded the definition of "general welfare" to mean any "government assistance or entitlement program" that the majority of Congress deems worthy is within Congress's jurisdiction. However, the 10th Amendment says otherwise: "The Powers not delegated to the United States by The Constitution, nor prohibited by it to the States, are reserved to the States respectively, or to the people."

It is clear that the Founders were specific that only those powers enumerated in the Constitution are enforceable. As further proof that our Founders were only giving the federal government certain, enumerated powers, one needs to read *The Federalist Papers* as it provides insight into what the Founders were thinking when they created the Constitution and were trying to get it ratified by the states.

From "Federalist 41" written by James Madison:

"It has been urged and echoed, that the power to 'to lay and collect taxes, duties, imposts, and excises, to pay the debts and provide for the common defense and general welfare of the United States,' amounts to an unlimited commission to exercise every power which may be alleged to be necessary for the common defense or general welfare. No stronger proof could be given of the distress under which these writers labor for objections, than their stooping to such a misconstruction." Misconstruction was defined by Webster in 1828 to be a "wrong interpretation of words; a mistaking of the true meaning."

"For what purpose could the enumeration of particular powers be inserted, if these and all others were meant to be included in the preceding general power? Nothing is more natural nor common than first to use a general phrase, and then to explain and qualify it by a recital of particulars. But the idea of an enumeration of particulars which neither explain nor qualify the general meaning, and can have no other effect than to confound and mislead, is an absurdity ...."

From "Federalist 45" written by James Madison:

"The powers delegated by the proposed Constitution to the federal government are few and defined. Those which are to remain in the State governments are numerous and indefinite. The former will be exercised principally on external objects, as war, peace, negotiation, and foreign commerce; with which last the power of taxation will, for the most part, be connected. The powers reserved to the several States will extend to all the objects which, in the ordinary course of affairs, concern the lives, liberties, and properties of the people."

From "Federalist 83," written by Alexander Hamilton:

"The plan of the convention declares that the power of Congress, or, in other words, of *national legislature*, shall extend to certain enumerated cases. This specification of particulars evidently excludes all pretension to a general legislative authority, because an affirmative grant of special powers would be absurd, as well as useless, if the general authority was intended."

Our federal government's blatant disregard of our Founders' wishes, as written in the Constitution, has created a bloated government with debt in excess of $19 trillion. More on that shortly, but for now remember that all of our federally elected officials, other than president, take the following oath: "I do solemnly swear (or affirm) that I will support and defend the Constitution of the United States against all enemies, foreign and domestic; that I will bear true faith and allegiance to the same; that I take this obligation freely, without any mental reservation or purpose of evasion; and that I will well and faithfully discharge the duties of the office on which I am about to enter. So help me God."

The president's oath is slightly different and is stated in the Constitution: "I do solemnly swear (or affirm) that I will faithfully execute the Office of President of the United States, and will to the best of my Ability, preserve, protect and defend the Constitution of the United States."

I guess the oath of adhering to the Constitution hasn't worked out as originally planned.

Chapter 9
What Has the Disregard of the Constitution Cost Us?

You should note that the United States government's source of revenue—the revenue meant to provide us with what is promised (refer to list in previous chapter)—is the taxation of American citizens and corporations doing business here. The government can't afford to provide us with anything unless it first taxes us. So, it really isn't the government giving you the benefits we all enjoy as citizens of this great country; it is *We the People* each contributing a portion of our hard-earned income for the benefit of all.

Our government is supposed to act as the steward of our money and is tasked with managing it properly so all its obligations, and no more, can be met. It is not technically legal for the government to provide more than what was promised in the Constitution, unless an amendment to the Constitution is passed. However, as I mentioned in the previous chapter, there have been times when Congress has refused to interpret the "general welfare" clause in the way our Founders intended, thus abusing its legal authority by spending money on its own pet projects and also creating "entitlement programs" such as Social Security, Medicare, and Medicaid that were enacted without Constitutional Amendments.

I am not saying these expenditures were all bad decisions, but they certainly weren't permitted by the "general welfare" clause or any other clause in the Constitution. What I am saying is that if we were to have these projects and programs, there should have been amendments made to the Constitution along the way.

Because of the government's mismanagement of our funds, our country is over $19 trillion in debt, not including what some claim to be over $50 trillion of unfunded liabilities to cover the future costs of "entitlement programs." This debt carries an annual interest payment which the government can either pay out of current cash flow from our taxes, or which it can pay by borrowing even more. Our government has chosen the latter as just a few years ago our debt was $15 trillion.

This debt is created when the government issues Treasury bills (less than one year maturity), notes (one to ten year maturity), and bonds (over ten year maturity). A little over 34% of our country's debt is owned by foreign countries, with China and Japan owning the most with around 7% each.[27] Foreign countries look to the United States as a "safe haven" for their money, particularly when there is turmoil in the world. I have been on this earth over fifty-nine years, and there always seems to have been some kind of turmoil, so I am confident foreign countries will continue to invest in our country. According to Paul Krugman in a January 1, 2012 *New York Times* op-ed, we should not fear foreign-owned debt because "America actually earns more from its assets abroad than it pays to foreign investors."[28]

Of the approximately 65 percent that is owned domestically, Social Security, the Federal Reserve, and other government agencies account for the majority (41% of the overall national debt, according to FactCheck.org in November of 2013).[29] The rest is owned by state and local governments, mutual funds, private pension funds, savings bonds, Treasury notes, banks, insurance companies, trusts, companies, and investors.

Folks, since our government only derives its money from us, it is really each of us who is on the hook for our country's interest payments and debt. It is obvious we, and more importantly our future generations, have a big problem because of our government's failure to abide by the Constitution and its "spending gone wild ways." When will the insanity end?

I am only one of many who are concerned about our country's spending habits and debt. As Senator Barrack H. Obama said in March, 2006, "The fact that we are here today to debate raising America's debt limit is a sign of leadership failure. It is a sign that the U.S. Government cannot pay its own bills. It is a sign that we now depend on ongoing assistance from foreign countries to finance our Government's reckless fiscal policies.... Increasing America's debt weakens us domestically and internationally. Leadership means that, 'the buck stops here.' Instead, Washington is shifting the burden of bad choices today onto the backs of our children and grandchildren. America has a debt problem and a failure of leadership. America deserves better."[30]

Unfortunately, the national debt has skyrocketed under President Obama's watch. Not all of it is his fault, nor is it all the fault of the Congress that served during his two terms—a significant portion in the increase in debt has been to fund programs put into place prior to his administration taking office. However, he and those serving in Congress should have gotten us on the right path by coming up with a plan to balance the annual budget and reduce our federal debt, rather than add to the problem.

We are fortunate that interest rates are currently very low, but they won't stay low forever. Eventually they will go up, and for each 1% rise in interest rates, our government will be obligated to pay an additional $190 billion per year with our tax money. We can't keep adding to our debt for much longer; we need to elect Congressional leaders who understand our country's financial strain, who are more concerned about doing what is right for the country than getting re-elected, and who are willing to make the tough fiscal decisions needed to get us out of this mess.

Chapter 10
Time to Heed President Kennedy's Call to Action

"Ask not what your country can do for you; ask what you can do for your country." Those famous words spoken by President Kennedy seem to be forgotten by our citizens and our elected officials, as it appears both have abdicated their responsibilities. Our citizens expect our government to provide a myriad of costly benefits and services that it (we) can't afford to the extent being provided. Unfortunately, many of our elected officials seem more concerned about being re-elected than they are about making the correct, but hard-to-sell, choices needed to prevent our country from continuing down the wrong financial path, like many countries in Europe have done.

I believe that if more Americans understood the severity of the financial situation we face, our elected officials would be less afraid of being booted out of office for making the sort of decisions that, though tough, would be correct, and which would assure the financial well-being of ourselves and our future generations. To accomplish this, our federally elected officials, all armed with the same audited data, should be mandated to hold town forums to educate their constituents about our country's finances. I am certainly not an expert in this area, but I do know some alarming facts:

1. According to the Department of Treasury (October, 2015), the government spent $3.688 trillion in the fiscal year 2015 that ended on September 30, with revenue of $3.249 trillion. This resulted in a budget deficit of $439 billion that added to our debt.[31]

2. According to the Congressional Budget Office (January 2016), 62% of the expenditures went to mandatory spending, which consists primarily of benefit programs for which laws set eligibility rules and benefit formulas. These include such things as Social Security, Medicare, Medicaid, unemployment compensation, federal civilian and military retirement, some veterans' benefits, the earned income tax credit, the Supplemental Nutrition Assistance Program, and other

mandatory programs, minus income from offsetting receipts. This equated to nearly $2.3 trillion.[32]

3. Thirty-two percent of the expenditures went for discretionary spending, which consists of spending that lawmakers control through annual appropriation acts, such as certain programs related to defense, transportation, education, veterans' benefits, health, housing assistance, and other activities. This equated to approximately $1.2 trillion.[33]

4. Six percent was for the Net Interest, which consists of the government's interest payments on debt held by the public, offset by interest income the government receives. This equated to $223 billion.[34] *Just remember what I said the number would be if interest rates went up just 1%, an extra $190 billion per year. Ouch!*

Over the last several decades, mandatory spending for Medicare and Social Security has continued to become an ever larger portion of our federal budget, and it will continue to grow even larger with our aging population. Without reform, we will likely see an increasing federal debt. This would not be a good scenario. The Congressional Budget Office states that "Large and growing amounts of federal debt over the coming decades would have negative long-term consequences for the economy and would constrain future budget policy. In particular, the projected amounts of debt would:

1. Reduce national saving and income in the long term;

2. Increase the government's interest costs, putting more pressure on the rest of the budget;

3. Limit lawmakers' ability to respond to unforeseen events; and

4. Make a fiscal crisis more likely."[35]

With a population more informed about our country's financial affairs, I believe the majority of our citizens would be willing to ask less from our government. This way, future generations could live in a country not riddled with debt—debt so high that it would require almost all of one's hard-earned income to simply pay off the accumulating interest while ensuring that no benefits could be received in return: no Social Security, no Medicare, no Medicaid, no anything. Some would counter that growing the Gross Domestic Product (GDP), which is a total of all the goods and services our nation produces each year, would negate the severity of the impact of a rising national debt and an aging population, but they cannot guarantee our nation will grow enough to make the problem insignificant. Right now we are struggling to produce two percent growth, so changes in our spending habits are certainly needed.

What you can do today for your country: Demand that Congress be honest with us about our country's finances—again, it is our money, not theirs—and take the time to do some studying on this subject; vote for people who are financially prudent yet compassionate, and who have a plan for those in society who cannot provide for themselves; if mentally and physically able, take responsibility for your own financial affairs; and finally, follow President Kennedy's advice so your children and children's children can have the freedoms you have enjoyed—freedoms only possible in a free country, not one beholden to those who purchased our debt.

Chapter 11
Time for a Thorough Government Audit

In order to turn around our nation's financial troubles, we need to appoint a commission with excellent financial acumen and strong leadership to analyze and reorganize, if necessary, all government departments and agencies. We need a thorough audit, similar to what President Truman and President Eisenhower had done when they both appointed former President Hoover to lead such commissions. The commissions were successful as numerous changes were subsequently instituted.

With over $19 trillion of debt and over $50 trillion of unfunded liabilities for future Social Security and Medicare costs, we can't just sit back and do nothing. I would appoint someone like David Walker, former Comptroller General of the United States (basically our nation's certified public accountant), to lead this commission. Few people understand our nation's finances better than he, and he is more concerned with *fiscal responsibility* than placating political parties. The plan he and his commission devise will then, according to law, need to be submitted to Congress for review, revision, and approval. If Congress can find and agree on someone more qualified than Mr. Walker to lead the commission, great. I just want the right plan for America and do not care who is in charge.

So, what is necessary for our government to continue funding? First, since it is clear that our government's main objective is to protect the citizens of our great country and our way of life, we need to fund a strong military, one that is the most advanced and makes all others fear us. Why so strong? To deter other countries from declaring war on us and our allies who espouse to the same belief in individual freedoms. A strong military is not meant for imperialistic pursuits; it is not our job to change the world, although it would be nice if every country believed their citizens deserved the freedoms we have. A strong military is for protection only.

If you question the need to fund a strong military, please read George Washington's farewell address that he gave to the nation on

September 19, 1796, after serving two terms as president of our great country. It is filled with sage advice such as reminding us "that timely disbursements to prepare for danger frequently prevent much greater disbursements to repel it."[36] You will also find his thoughts regarding our national debt; foreign influence; the need for a religious, moral, and educated citizenry; and his fear about political parties to be interesting, insightful, and very applicable for the challenges we face today.

Second, given the fact that we are over $19 trillion in debt, I believe we have an obligation to pay the annual interest on our debt and devise a plan to reduce it. Third, we need to fund infrastructure programs to make sure that we can travel safely and help reduce the transportation costs businesses incur. Fourth, we need to fund our court system, so our individual rights are protected. Fifth, we need to fund departments that insure the regulations created by Congress to protect the "general welfare of the United States," as defined by the Framers of the Constitution—not today's elected officials—are carried out. Examples would be departments to oversee strong, but not onerous, banking and securities regulations so we can be assured our savings and investments are not being mishandled, and environmental protection regulations so we have clean air and water. Sixth, we need to fund departments or agencies that complement our military and local police departments, such as the FBI, NSA, Secret Service, and CIA. And seventh, even though in my opinion they were unconstitutional when created, we need to fund our "entitlement programs" (Social Security and Medicare) because too many people today are reliant upon them for economic survival. It would be foolish and unfair to think they can be stopped in the near-term. However, we must come up with a plan so we don't put our children's future in financial peril. Based on our Constitution, I believe it is clear that our federal government should not be involved in education and many other things it gets its nose into. That is why we have states.

It is obvious that we need a plan to put our country on the right financial path. However, it should be equally obvious that the plan needs to be structured in a morally sound way. Our government can't stop funding all programs that many believe to be unconstitutional. Nor can it reduce a large number of its employees all at once in order to save on payroll costs. Many Americans who either rely on these programs or rely on the government for employment would be financially devastated if this were to occur. Because of this, any changes recommended by the commission must be implemented in a compassionate, humane way that will more than likely take many years to fully institute. And that is okay—as long as we get on the right path immediately.

Chapter 12
Is Economic Success Still Achievable by the Masses?

When you see the tremendous amount of income inequality in our nation today, you might question whether economic success is still achievable. What you must realize is that each person has his or her own definition of economic success; we each have different needs and wants. We are not all going to make the *Forbes* 400 list of wealthiest people, but that doesn't make us failures. To me, economic success is having enough income, generated through work, savings and investments, to live the life I choose. Yes, I would like more income, but it would not be right to feel that I deserve more than I earned and saved. Rest assured that we all have the opportunity for economic success, but our chances diminish if we don't have the right factors working in our favor.

In *Wealth, Poverty and Politics,* Thomas Sowell provides a history lesson about why each of us, no matter what country we come from or the color of our skin, either succeeds economically or doesn't. Geographic factors, cultural factors, social factors, and political factors are the main determinants; genetic determinism is not. Over thousands of years of recorded history, there have been major disparities in people's standards of living. Dr. Sowell says: "These disparities have extended beyond wealth to the things that create wealth, including the knowledge, skills, habits and discipline that have developed unequally in different geographic, cultural, and political settings."[37]

Geography has played a role from the beginning of time as some parts of the world lived in isolation because either they couldn't easily be reached or the climate prevented them from cultivating and creating anything of value to trade or disease ran rampant. It is easy to understand how isolation has set some people and nations back economically, culturally, and socially. According to Dr. Sowell, "The fate of whole races, nations, and civilizations can depend on whether they happen to be located in the right place at the right time or in the wrong place at the wrong time."[38]

Dr. Sowell states that cultures include customs, values, attitudes, skills, and talents that directly affect economic output. Economists refer to these as *human capital.* "To account for the radical differences in income and wealth among groups living in the same society, environment can be defined as what is going on *around* a group, while culture means what is going on *within* each group."[39] When people from a group leave one area for another, they take their culture with them, and for this reason they cannot expect the same income and wealth as people from another group in the same area that have a more advanced culture.

However, it is possible for a group to elevate its culture over time. Being *receptive* to the cultures of more advanced groups (i.e. races; nations) can speed up the process. Dr. Sowell points out that Japan benefitted when, after centuries of lagging behind China, it became culturally receptive to aspects of the Chinese culture that helped Japan become more productive in industry and in the creation of their own written language. He also points out that by not translating a higher percentage of the world's books into Arabic, the Arab world has not helped advance its roughly 300 million people as much as it could have.[40]

To earn a good income, one must be able to produce something others, including an employer, want and will pay for. And in order to produce something, one must acquire and continue to develop one's human capital in order to improve one's marketable skills. How does one do that? Be culturally receptive by committing to be a life-long learner of the skills necessary for economic success, and be an ethical, honest, polite, hard-working, trustworthy person.

As Dr. Sowell writes, the social factors that can affect economic differences between nations and within nations include the demographics of the population, and the human capital and social mobility in their societies. If the median age of one group is older than that of another, the older age group is likely to earn more income and have greater wealth because as people age, they improve their communication skills and develop better marketable skills.[41]

Dr. Sowell believes that the quantity of words children hear, and both the quantity and quality of their parents, have a significant impact on children: "A study [by *The Economist* magazine] found that American children in families where the parents are in professional occupations hear 2,100 words an hour, on average. Children whose parents are working class hear an average of 1,200 an hour—and children whose family is on welfare hear 600 words per hour. What this means is that, over the years, a ten-year-old child from a family on welfare will have heard not quite as many words at home as a three-year-old child whose parents are professionals."[42] The lack of a wide vocabulary, of course, makes it harder for poor children to fit in socially and get educated to their full potential, which in turn makes it harder for them to achieve economic success.

Interestingly, the study also showed that "only 9 percent of American women with college degrees who gave birth in 2013 were unmarried. But 61 percent of women who were high school dropouts and gave birth that year were unmarried."[43] Dr. Sowell, like so many others, believes that children raised by both a mother and a father have a much better chance in life.

The conclusion of the study was that although children who are born into a poor household have an *equal opportunity*, they do not have *equal life chances* for success. This all goes back to my premise that we need to improve our educational system, particularly in poor neighborhoods, so these children have a better chance of economic success and happiness—something every child in America deserves.

Dr. Sowell, a black man, argues that social changes starting in the 1960s have hurt the economic chances in the portion of the black community that celebrates what he refers to as a *ghetto culture* and "an offshoot of the dysfunctional redneck culture of the South, though often regarded as something uniquely black or even African, despite much evidence to the contrary, [and that] so-called black English has no connection with languages in Africa but very strong connections with the way English was spoken, centuries ago, in the parts of Britain from which white Southerners came."[44]

Over the years, many black children have felt the need to grasp on to this so-called ghetto culture as it pertains to attitude, values, and behavior so they can *fit-in* and not be accused of *acting white* and subjecting themselves to the potential for ridicule, ostracism, threats and physical abuse.

Dr. Sowell quotes legendary basketball star Kareem Abdul-Jabbar's description of growing up in this type of culture: "I got all A's and was hated for it; I spoke correctly and was called a punk. I had to learn a new language simply to be able to deal with the threats. I had good manners and was a good little boy and paid for it with my hide."[45] What my first college basketball hero had to go through is sad; even sadder is that many of today's youngsters are going through the same thing.

Unfortunately, speaking proper English, a prerequisite for getting a good paying job unless you are a rapper or professional athlete, is looked down upon in certain black circles—you will be accused of acting white. How is that being culturally receptive? How is this mentality helping these individuals attain economic success? I think the message is clear: Follow those who came before you that have succeeded by getting a good education, working hard, and creating a great family environment.

Political factors can also be a hurdle in our quest for economic success. Political battling has gone on throughout history, and this has caused the persecution of many productive groups of people, and sent some of them economically backwards for long periods of time.

Today in the United States, we have seen two political parties doing anything possible to win elections. Between the lies, name calling, and accusations that those less fortunate are victims of those who are more fortunate, it has become an ugly mess that has helped to create a polarized country. I guess all this shouldn't be a surprise, because given how much money can be made, many politicians today will say and do anything to get elected; and when they retire after a long political career, they can make even more money on the speaking circuit or working for a lobbying firm. As I said earlier, term limits would be a good solution.

Dr. Sowell warns us to be careful of politicians seeking votes, and those in racially or ethnically motivated leadership roles who offer people from economically disadvantaged groups the following:[46]

1. Assurance that their [group's situation] is not their fault.
2. Assurance that their [group's situation is] the fault of [a more well off] group that they already envy and resent.
3. Assurance that [their group's] culture is just as good as anybody else's, if not better.
4. Assurance that what [their] group needs and deserves is a demographically defined "fair share" of the economic and

other benefits of society, sometimes supplemented with some kind of reparations for past injustices or some special reward for being indigenous "sons of the soil."

This type of rhetoric fans the flames of discontent and only benefits the one offering lies and empty promises. It does nothing to bring about needed change and unify us as a nation. If we all thought about ourselves as Americans first and less about our heritage and its unique customs, and concentrated more on our similarities and being civil toward one another, we would have a better chance of living in a more peaceful and prosperous society. To succeed economically every American needs to, no matter what their heritage, do the following:

1. Master the English language.
2. Get a good education and develop the skills and behaviors necessary to be a productive member of society.
3. Develop a strong work ethic.
4. Provide their children with a loving family atmosphere.
5. Follow the Golden Rule: Do unto others as you would have them do unto you.

For all who do those things, economic success is still achievable!

Chapter 13
Income Inequality

Even though there is a formula for achieving economic success, some people claim that the disparity in incomes in our country is proof that the system is rigged in favor of the "top 1%" and that the opportunity for economic success is not available to us all. According to a January 26, 2015 article in the *Huffington Post*, the Economic Policy Institute, a nonprofit, nonpartisan think tank created in 1986 to include low and moderate income workers in economic policy discussions, declared that to make the top 1% of earners in Arkansas, you needed an income of $228,298 per year, and in Connecticut, $677,608 per year.[47]

I live in Connecticut and wish I made over $677,000 per year. Good thing you don't need that much income to be an economic success. Remember, it is your definition of economic success that matters, not what the media tells us.

Columbia University professor Joseph Stiglitz wrote a book entitled *The Price of Inequality* that addresses why he believes the economic division in this country between the rich and the poor is endangering our future. He speaks generally about the top 1%, but to his credit, he explains that his real problem is with the top 1/10 of 1% of wage earners. Dr. Stiglitz believes that many business leaders, particularly bankers, have lost their moral compass, and he blames capitalism for much it.[48] I disagree with him that capitalism can be blamed for the cause of one's moral decay. There have been greedy and morally depraved people throughout history, and some of the biggest offenders have been leaders of socialist and totalitarian regimes. He also no longer sees America as the land of opportunity we once were.[49] As stated earlier, there are hurdles we all have to overcome, but the opportunity is still there.

I do, however, believe that Dr. Stiglitz and I are in agreement on a number of points:

1. Many CEOs of large publicly owned companies get paid too much because they answer to a Board of Directors, often handpicked, rather than to shareholders.

2. Executives taking pay raises doesn't seem justified when, if at the same time, they are firing workers to reduce wage costs.

3. There are periods when markets fail to produce efficient and desirable outcomes, and there is a role for government in correcting these market failures; that is, designing policies (taxes and regulations) that bring private incentives and social returns into alignment.

4. Companies selling products to our government at above market prices must not be allowed.

5. It costs too much to run for political office, and we are in need of campaign finance reform. I am sure we are missing out on some terrific candidates who just can't afford to run for office.

6. With the *Citizens United* court case, the Supreme Court essentially approved unbridled corporate campaign spending, and this was not a good decision. Too much power goes to those who control the money.

7. We must increase demand for goods and services, and to accomplish that we need *We the People* with more disposable income. A more business friendly environment where wage increases would be possible and a revamped tax code would both help accomplish this.

Although there are instances where the less educated and poor have been taken advantage of by those with more substantial means, the more common reasons for one's lack of economic success have been the factors discussed earlier. Thomas Sowell put it this way: "If the less fortunate peoples of the world are less fortunate primarily because they are victims of the more fortunate, then the goal to pursue in trying to make things right can be very different from what the goal would be if the less fortunate are seen as people lacking the geographic, cultural and other advantages enjoyed by others, largely through no fault of theirs or of others."[50] So it really comes down to which problem is more important to solve:

1. The reduction or elimination of economic gaps between people, or

2. Spreading prosperity to all people by making sure everyone has the opportunity to learn the skills and behaviors necessary for economic success.

Many people may feel the above are complementary goals and want to accomplish both. However, consider this: If everyone's skills were improved and their income doubled—which would be a good thing if purchasing power remained the same because it would reduce the number of people living in poverty—it would increase the income inequality in the world. Given that scenario, I would argue that finding a way to spread prosperity is a more important goal than one that attempts to solve the income inequality issue. That said, I believe the compensation of CEOs at the world's largest corporations is too high in relation to the value they provide their respective companies, and excessive in relation to the pay of rank and file employees.

Since those who lack the most basic things in life would certainly benefit the most from improved skills and a rise in income, I believe our government's efforts should be channeled in this direction, and less on income inequality.

A couple things you should note:

1. Income disparity is not always the best indicator of economic disparity. Standard of living is a better indicator. According to Dr. Sowell, "In the United States, most households in the lowest 20 percent of income recipients have *no one* working. Most of the economic resources transferred to them are transferred in kind, such as subsidized housing, medical care and other such benefits, rather than money. Therefore disparities expressed in money income statistics greatly exaggerate disparities in standards of living, especially for people living in what the welfare state chooses to define as poverty."[51]

2. Dr. Sowell argues that the majority of statistical studies regarding income trends are not the most accurate. One type of study breaks down into quintiles the income levels of the population each year and then compares the data with other years. This study is straightforward and easy to calculate as there is no concern for the fact that there is an ever changing mix of people in each quintile. Statistics from this study are what the media, politicians, and academic world most often cite. Dr. Sowell believes the other type of study, which follows the changes of the annual income of identical individuals over many years, is more costly but a more accurate measure as to

what is happening with people's incomes. Why is this? Because people move from one quintile to another in the normal course of their careers, getting paid much more once they are experienced than when they started out. Logically, people in their 50s and 60s normally get paid a lot more than someone in their 20s.[52] I think it is obvious that the second type of study gives a more accurate assessment of where our population is economically.

There will always be some people who make better use of their opportunities than others. Given that, one cannot expect to have equality of outcomes. However, this is a good thing because being able to benefit and prosper from freedom of opportunity is the main reason our ancestors came to America.

Chapter 14
Minimum Wage

There is a lot of debate about whether it would be a good idea to raise the minimum wage. As I mentioned earlier, I agree with Dr. Stiglitz's belief that we need employee income to increase. However, I am not convinced that a higher minimum wage is the answer.

In a January 30, 2014 article in *Forbes*, Jeffrey Dorfman shared some information from the Bureau of Labor Statistics: "There are about 3.6 million workers at or below the minimum wage (you can be below legally under certain conditions, such as people who make tips in addition to a wage). That is 2.5 percent of all workers, [and] within that small group, 31 percent are teenagers and 55 percent are 25 years old or younger, [a group that is just starting out in the work force and not supporting a family.] That leaves about 1.1 percent of all workers over 25 earning the minimum wage."[53] Today, approximately 66 percent of those making minimum wage are in the service industry, and close to half work in food services.

Mr. Dorfman also talked about and disproves a study touted by the Left claiming "that if the minimum wage had risen in tandem with worker productivity, the minimum wage would be nearly $22 per hour."[54] He continues: "Labor productivity may have risen faster than the minimum wage over the last twenty or thirty years, but the study getting all the press uses the productivity gains of all workers to calculate a hypothetical increase in the minimum wage. What is needed is a measure of productivity gains of the minimum wage workers. Unfortunately, the government does not produce such a number."[55]

What the Bureau of Labor Statistics does track is the labor productivity of food service workers, which represents 44 percent of all minimum wage earners. Mr. Dorfman believes this is a fair proxy for the group as a whole, and the data show that in 2011 there were no productivity gains and there was a 0.1 percent drop in 2012. "Taking a longer view, from 1987 to 2012 the same BLS data show that worker productivity in the food service sector rose by an average of 0.6 percent per year." Over this period, the minimum wage increased 3.1

percent per year, and as Mr. Dorfman says, "at a rate five to six times as fast as justified by the gains in worker productivity."[56] Obviously, the study suggesting productivity gains warrant a $22 minimum wage is incorrect.

A few other things to consider when you hear of a proposal to increase to the minimum wage:

1. Minimum wage workers usually earn a higher wage within a short period of time, after they gain some experience and prove they add value to the organization.

2. In many cases, an increase in the minimum wage results in increased customer prices.

3. The discussion is most often brought up near elections because many union contracts are tied to a multiple of the minimum wage. Since unions contribute heavily during political campaigns, they have the influence to often get this subject on the political agenda.

Please note that when you hear a politician suggest a higher minimum wage, it may not be for benevolent reasons. It may be for campaign contributions and votes. If you know someone only earning the minimum wage, refer them to Chapter 12, "Is Economic Success Still Achievable by the Masses?" for a prescription on how to earn an hourly rate well in excess of the minimum wage.

Chapter 15
Our Over-Regulated Society

Our Founders, many of whom were great students of history, formed a representative form of government with three branches (Executive, Legislative, and Judicial) so there would be a *separation of powers* and *checks and balances* to protect *We the People* from too strong a central government. James Madison, our fourth president and chief architect of the Constitution, wrote in "Federalist 51": "If men were angels, no government would be necessary. If angels were to govern men, neither external nor internal controls on government would be necessary." Since we are only human, we need controls, the controls our Founders instituted.

Thomas Jefferson said in his First Inaugural address: "A wise and frugal government, which shall restrain men from injuring one another, shall leave them otherwise free to regulate their own pursuits of industry and improvement, and shall not take from the mouth of labor the bread it has earned. This is the sum of good government."[57]

Today, we apparently have gotten away from the small, limited government with built-in protections, as our federal government has grown in size and complexity—and is so over-regulated that it has hurt the growth of our economy. Many of these regulations have come from what some call the "fourth branch of government," *administrative agencies* with a great deal of power, supposedly headed by people of tremendous wisdom in their field of expertise. Administrative Agencies include organizations such as the Environmental Protection Agency (EPA), Consumer Financial Protection Bureau CFPB), Federal Trade Commission (FTC), Drug Enforcement Administration (DEA), and many, many more. We need to be careful of these administrative agencies that have been dictating "law" for quite some time without being required to answer to our elected officials in Congress. In the last paragraph of Article 1, Section 8 of the United States Constitution, it states that Congress has the power "to make Laws which shall be necessary and proper for carrying into Execution the foregoing Powers, and all other Powers vested by this Constitution in the Government of the United States, or in any Department or Officer thereof." It does not say that our elected officials can abdicate their responsibilities, and it does not say that these departments/agencies do not have to follow our system of *checks and balances* and report to Congress and the president, which together have the ultimate responsibility for creating and carrying out law.

In the second paragraph of the Declaration of Independence, it states that "Governments are instituted among Men, deriving their just powers from the consent of the governed." In our system of government, *We the People*, the governed, are given the sovereign power by having the right to vote Congress in and out of office. Voting is our means of *checks and balances*, just like our three branches have *checks and balances* on each other. Our nation was set up so that no person or branch of government would ever have an excessive amount of power. Remember the saying, "Power corrupts; absolute power corrupts absolutely."

It is time for our elected officials to reign in these administrative agencies, take back control, and give us only the amount of regulations necessary for our freedom, our safety, our right to clean air and water, and our ability to conduct business within a fair, ethical playing field.

According to a February 18, 2012 article in *The Economist*, "A study done by the Small Business Administration, a government body, found that regulations in general add $10,585 in costs per employee."[58] That is a lot of money an employer has to earn in order to break even. Don't think for a minute that this doesn't affect hiring practices and wages.

In *You Know I'm Right*, Michelle Caruso-Cabrera expressed her thoughts on over-regulation: "In the effort to make something better for a tiny part of the population, the entire population suffers. We see this over and over again, whether it's in education, health care, or air service."[59]

Obviously, all societies need laws and regulations. However, many of ours are just plain ridiculous and costly. *The Economist* article mentioned a few:[60]

1. A Florida law requiring vending machine labels to urge the public to file a report if the label is not there.

2. The Federal Railroad Administration insists that all trains must be painted with an "F" at the front, so you can tell which end is which.

3. In Bethesda, Maryland, children's lemonade stands have been shut down because they did not have trading licenses.

The journalist made the observation that "Americans are supposed to be free to choose, for better or for worse. Yet for some time America has been straying from this ideal."[61] He also pointed out that there are two forces that make American laws too complex:[62]

1. Many lawmakers believe they can lay down rules to govern every eventuality. However, complexity creates loopholes that the shrewd can abuse with impunity.

2. Complex lobbying. The government's drive to micromanage so many activities creates a huge incentive for interest groups to push for special favors. When a bill is hundreds of pages long, it is not hard for congressmen to slip in clauses that benefit their chums and campaign donors.

When you look at the length and complexity of Dodd-Frank and the Affordable Care Act (Obamacare), you know that regulation has gone too far. The article in *The Economist* went on to say that "America needs a smarter approach to regulation. First, all important rules should be subjected to cost-benefit analysis by an independent watchdog. The results should be made public before the rule can be enacted. All big regulations should also come with sunset clauses, so that they expire after, say, ten years unless Congress explicitly re-authorizes them. More important, rules need to be much simpler. When regulators try to write an all-purpose instruction manual, the truly important dos and don'ts are lost in an ocean of verbiage. Far better to lay down broad goals and prescribe only what is strictly necessary to achieve them. Legislators should pass simple rules and leave regulators to enforce them. Would this hand too much power to unelected bureaucrats? Not if they are made more accountable."[63]

The authors of the well-respected *Economist* must have read "Federalist 62" and are familiar with how our country is supposed to be run. James Madison writes: "It will be of little avail to the people, that the laws are made by men of their own choice, if the laws be so voluminous that they cannot be read, or so incoherent that they cannot be understood."

Time to get back to our Founders' government!

Chapter 16
Term Limits

The president of the United States can serve a maximum of two four-year terms. Senators serve a six-year term with no restrictions on the number of terms. Representatives serve a two-year term with no restrictions on the number of terms. Do you think it is possible that, at times, our elected officials will make promises they know they cannot keep, or that they might vote for a piece of legislation that, though they know isn't in the country's best interest, will make them look good "back home" and help their chances of getting re-elected? Do you think it is possible that someone running for office for the first time will also make promises they know they cannot keep if elected? It's not only possible, it happens all the time.

Many of our elected officials, both Democrats and Republicans, also manipulate the truth in order to make it seem that they are the only ones who can protect their constituents. A good example of this was several years ago, when I read in the newspaper that an elected official in Connecticut spoke to a group of seniors and led them to believe that they were in danger of losing Medicare benefits. They were told that the plans on the table "ask the deepest sacrifice of our seniors" and "the proposed Medicare changes would drastically affect seniors' quality of life as payment provided by the government through the plan likely wouldn't be enough to cover their health care costs."

This was not true because no healthcare proposal on the table at that time was to affect anyone over the age of fifty-five. My grandmother, who was 104 years old at the time, and I were not concerned that she was going to lose any of her benefits. This is just one example of politicians playing into the public's fears.

A few years ago, this same elected official refused to review a tax article that I wrote, even though it was given to her by one of her close political allies, who had read it and thought highly of it. I was told by our mutual friend that, although I was a constituent, the elected official refused to look at it because I was not affiliated with her party. Who cares what side of the aisle a good idea comes from? Apparently, many of our elected officials do, and that is sad. And I guess I'm not the only one to have had this problem when their elected official is from a different party. Greg Orman, successful business person and former Independent candidate for U.S. senator in Kansas, wrote in his book *A Declaration of Independents* that "Many voters would find it difficult to engage in a constructive problem-solving dialogue with a candidate or officeholder of a party different from theirs. Their filters and conditioning would make it difficult for them to actively listen and seek out common ground."[64] For our nation to become all that it can be, these narrow-minded people must no longer be elected into office.

It is time for fiscal responsibility, not plans that just sound good so one can get elected or re-elected. Term limits would make telling the truth a lot easier for politicians as no one would be worried about maintaining a lifetime job. And it would help make lobbyists much less powerful.

Because there are no term limits for elected officials other than the president, we as a nation have made it too easy to make politics a career. We need good pragmatic people in office who are willing to serve the country's interests, not their own. I think we should consider having twelve years as the maximum time members of the House of Representative and Senate can serve. Some people have suggested the idea of a one-term presidency of six years. That may not be a bad idea given how campaigns can get messy and time consuming.

When the Constitution was written, the only federal election *We the People* were allowed to directly vote in was for our district's member in the U.S. House of Representatives. Citizens did not get to vote directly for U.S. senators or the president. Senators were chosen by state legislatures that were elected by *We the People*, and presidents were elected by electors appointed by state legislatures. Wondering why our Founders designed only a two-year term for members of the U.S. House of Representatives? Because it gave *We the People* a way to vote bad representatives out of office after only a short period of time.

As for term limits, some will complain that we need people with experience down in Washington. With the gridlock and no side willing to compromise, that hasn't worked out too well for us recently. Plus, if we get back to the limited form of government that our country was founded upon, we shouldn't need any career politicians. We need good thinkers and stewards rotating in and out. And this will eliminate the need to pay for elaborate healthcare and retirement programs for those who serve.

Chapter 17
Tax Code

Because of the complexity of the U.S. Tax Code, it is obvious that it is in need of some major changes, both on the corporate side and the individual side. Frankly, changes on the corporate side should take priority. Why? Because *We the People* actually pay the majority of the corporate taxes since any tax charged to a corporation is passed along to us via higher prices to consumers, lower wages to employees, and lower returns to shareholders.

With a more fair tax code, American multi-national companies would start bringing their money and jobs back to the United States, and that would be a good thing. Maybe we could even convince more foreign corporations to set up shop here. I propose a schedule with tax brackets of 10%, 15%, and 20% with fewer deductions, credits, and exclusions. This will be good for *We the People*. I will leave it up to more knowledgeable people to work out the particulars, including income breakpoint levels. However, I do have a couple suggestions.

I propose the elimination of "carried interest" getting special tax treatment. I fail to see why investment managers of *private equity funds* are allowed to have the income they earn from managing other people's money taxed at the more favorable capital gains rate rather than as ordinary income like the rest of us are on our earned income. I also propose that the elimination of stock options as a method of employee compensation be considered. This would help to simplify corporate tax reporting and put an end to an unnecessary tax benefit for the wealthy—the conversion of ordinary income into capital gains. My last thoughts about corporate taxes focus on employer-sponsored benefit plans, such as health insurance and retirement plans. Since they need a more detailed explanation, I will address them later in a separate chapter.

On the individual side, let's first take a look at the history of the income tax. President Lincoln imposed the first U.S. income tax in 1862 to help pay for the Civil War. It was repealed in 1885 when the Supreme Court declared income taxes to be unconstitutional. This decision stood until the ratification of the 16th Amendment in 1913, which gave Congress the power to "lay and collect taxes on incomes."

The tax rates in 1913 started at 1% on income up to $20,000 and increased gradually to a maximum of 7% on income greater than $500,000. According to the Bureau of Labor Statistics, $20,000 in 1913 has the purchasing power of $483,356 today and $500,000 has the purchasing power of $12,083,889. The Code was only fifteen pages; now it is over 3,500 pages.

We hear a lot about simplifying the tax code and having people pay their fair share. To me, simplifying the tax code has more to do with deductions and credits that attempt to direct behaviors than it does about the number of tax brackets. Personally, I do not see how a flat tax rate such as 10% is fair given that a 10% tax on someone earning $25,000 per year affects that person's power to purchase goods and services much more so than a 10% tax on someone earning $250,000 or $2,500,000 per year. Having said that, please note that having an income of $250,000 should not classify one as being rich, particularly if you live in an expensive part of the country, have a mortgage, are paying for your children's education, and are trying to save for retirement so you won't be a burden to society when you get older. Politicians who say someone earning $250,000 is rich are just doing so to garner votes from the uninformed.

Some people have proposed lowering tax rates and combining that with a consumption tax (tax on goods and services purchased). The opponents to that strategy come from two camps. One says that a consumption tax is regressive and hurts those with low incomes; although, most plans discussed would not tax necessities such as food and clothing and some plans would give a credit back to those with low incomes. The other camp has no faith in elected officials (can't blame them) and believes that, if we start with a small consumption tax, it will continue to be raised as our elected officials love to spend our hard-earned money.

If it is determined that the income tax is the best way for our country to generate revenue, I do not have a big problem continuing with our progressive tax rate structure, one that increases the tax rate as one's income rises, even though it has communist ties. Don't believe me? Check out chapter two in *The Communist Manifesto* by Karl Marx and Frederick Engels where they list ten things they require in their vison of the ideal social order, one of which is "a heavy progressive or graduated income tax."[65] We have had such a progressive income tax since 1913, and I assume we will for years to come.

If we are going to stay with a progressive tax structure, I would propose more brackets, not fewer. It doesn't make filing a tax return any more difficult, and it can be used to assist those in society who could use a tax break—the middle class. I would love to say that I have the magical rate formula, but I do not. Maybe the commission I proposed earlier in the pamphlet can come up with it. All I know is that any tax changes have to be revenue neutral until the commission can figure out where we can cut the budget and get us on track for balancing our budget and lowering our debt and unfunded future liabilities.

Below are our current tax rates for Married Filing Jointly and an alternative that shows more brackets, although I do not have enough information to determine how close it is to revenue neutral. The rationale for my attempt at a new rate structure centers around the following:

1. The middle class needs to be able to keep more of its income.

2. Owners of small-businesses provide the majority of jobs in this country and should not be burdened with excessive taxes that make it difficult for them to expand and create more good paying jobs, something our country desperately needs.

3. Since the majority of small-business owners make less than $500,000 per year, my alternative shows a tax savings for those making less than that, and an increase for those making more than that.

2016 Rates/Taxable Income		Alt. Rates/Taxable Income	
10%	$0 - $18,550	5%	$0 - $25,000
15%	$18,551 - $75,300	10%	$25,001 - $50,000
25%	$75,301 - $151,900	20%	$50,001 - $100,000
28%	$151,901 - $231,450	25%	$100,001 - $200,000
33%	$231,451 - $413,350	30%	$200,001 - $300,000
35%	$413,351 - $466,950	35%	$300,001 - $400,000

39.6%	$466,951 plus	40%	$400,001 - $500,000
		45%	$500,001 - $1,000,000
		50%	$1,000,001 plus

Let's now compare how much you would pay in taxes at several different income levels:

Taxable Income	2016 Tax	Alternative Tax
$25,000	$2,823	$1,250
$50,000	$6,573	$3,750
$75,000	$10,323	$8,750
$100,000	$16,543	$13,750
$125,000	$22,793	$20,000
$150,000	$29,043	$26,250
$175,000	$35,986	$32,500
$200,000	$42,986	$38,750
$250,000	$57,913	$53,750
$300,000	$74,413	$68,750
$400,000	$107,413	$103,750
$500,000	$143,666	$143,750
$600,000	$183,266	$188,750
$700,000	$222,866	$233,750
$800,000	$262,466	$278,750
$900,000	$302,066	$323,750
$1,000,000	$341,666	$368,750
$2,000,000	$737,666	$868,750
$5,000,000	$1,925,666	$2,368,750
$10,000,000	$3,905,666	$4,868,750
$20,000,000	$7,865,666	$9,868,750
$50,000,000	$19,745,666	$24,868,750

In addition to the change in tax rates in the alternative plan, I recommend the following provisions: 1) Capital gains be taxed as ordinary income with a 25% cap (investment in businesses should be encouraged, so a lower tax rate is beneficial to all Americans); 2) Dividends be tax deductible to the corporations paying the dividends and taxed as ordinary income to the recipients (wealthy people do not need a lower tax rate on dividends); 3) Continue allowing taxpayers to deduct the interest paid on first and second mortgages up to $1,000,000 in mortgage debt (combined total on main home and one second home). Although this directs behavior, as it incentivizes the purchase of a home versus renting, this is positive for society because, on average, homeowners take better care of their property and neighborhood than tenants; 4) Keep the favorable tax treatment for health insurance and retirement plans; 5) Eliminate the Alternative Minimum Tax; 6) Estates not be taxed on the first $10,000,000 of assets; over that institute a 20% tax (I do not believe that people who created an estate should have more than one-fifth of it "confiscated" at death). If $10,000,000 sounds too high before taxes kick-in, please note that at a 3% rate of return, it generates $300,000 per year, which is not a huge income; and 7) Bring back "income averaging" that was abolished in 1986 except for farmers, fisherman, and certain retirees cashing out of a qualified retirement plan. How is it fair that a person who earns a lot of money in one year and significantly less in other years, pays substantially more income taxes over a three to five year period than a person who earns the same total amount of money over the same period, but has a level income from year to year? Doesn't seem fair to me.

Naturally, there are many more households with low to moderate levels of income than there are ones making over $1,000,000 per year. Therefore, my guess is that the alternative I illustrated is not revenue neutral. If that is the case, we really need the commission I referenced sooner rather than later because the tax savings families making less than $500,000 per year would experience with the alternative plan is really not all that much.

It should be obvious that government spending needs to be curbed and our tax code needs to be amended. Remember that when you vote.

Chapter 18
Social Security

Social Security, one of the entitlement programs I spoke about earlier, was started in 1935 and is now counted on by a great many people to live comfortably during their retirement years. However, it was never supposed to be the sole source or even a large percentage of one's retirement income. It was supposed to be a safety net, and it was modeled after a plan German Chancellor Otto von Bismarck created in the 1870s to assist people in his country who lived longer than life expectancy, no longer worked, and needed money.

During the 1870s in Germany, life expectancy was age fifty-five. Bismarck's plan was designed to start paying benefits at age seventy, but was later switched to sixty-five. When Social Security started in 1935, even though Americans had a life expectancy of sixty-five, benefits started at sixty-five rather than sometime after life expectancy, like in Bismarck's plan.[66]

As you are aware, Social Security is funded by working Americans through a deduction from one's wages and employer contributions. It was designed for these deductions and contributions to go into an interest earning *trust fund*. According to David Walker, author of *Comeback America*, "This system worked fine in the early years of Social Security. America had a lot more workers than retired people, and the trust funds generated healthy surpluses."[67] The problem now is that baby boomers had fewer children than the previous generation with the result being that there are fewer workers paying into the system and more retirees than ever before receiving benefits. In other words, our Social Security system was not an actuarially sound plan from the beginning. It was certainly not as sound as Bismarck's plan.

What you may not know is that our government has used money in the trust fund to pay for other government programs. In the March 2015 issue of *Reason*, Michael D. Tanner wrote: "The so-called trust fund is simply an accounting measure, specifying how much money the federal government owes the program out of general revenues, not an actual asset that can be used to pay benefits."[68] Mr. Walker says in his book that the government has issued special U.S. government securities it owes to the trust fund that are really "government IOUs that the government issued to itself, to be paid back later—with interest."[69] He goes on to say that "under current federal accounting principles, the government does not consider these securities to be liabilities—which is another way of saying the government doesn't really think that it's our money."[70] That, of course, makes no sense because the government does, in fact, owe *We the People* the money.

Interestingly, although the government is not listing all the money we paid into Social Security as a liability, they are reporting these securities as assets on the annual reports they provide to the public. Mr. Walker and many others believe that what the government owes the trust fund for the benefit of *We the People* should be treated as a liability and the value should be counted as part of our country's debt-to-GDP ratio. The non-reporting of this liability makes the federal deficit look smaller than it actually is and adds to the growing unfunded future obligations.[71]

It's time for the government to be held to the same accounting standards as large corporations, and time for our elected officials to create an actuarially sound plan that won't burden future generations!

Chapter 19
Employer-Sponsored Benefit Plans

I believe employee benefit plans such as health insurance and retirement plans have hurt small businesses, large corporations, both municipal and state governments, and as a result, *We the People*. My idea, possibly my most controversial and not necessarily Centrist, is to get employers out of the "benefits business," which I believe would be a boon for employment and wages. Let's look at health insurance first.

To start, have you ever wondered why most of us get our health insurance from our employer and don't purchase it like we do our auto, home, and life insurance? Michelle Caruso-Cabrera writes: "It's the unintended consequence of bad government policies from World War II. During the war, in the 1940s, there was a severe labor shortage. The government thought it was doing everyone a favor by instituting wage controls and declaring that no company could pay more than any other company for workers. The government didn't want stronger companies taking advantage of weaker companies by paying more for employees. So what did the stronger companies do to attract workers they desperately needed? Industries and businesses that needed workers and had the financial resources began offering nonwage benefits such as health insurance. We've been stuck with it ever since. The strong companies ended up being able to attract employees anyway, which makes the entire concept of employer-based insurance a perfect example of well-intentioned government intervention that fails to achieve the desired effect and in fact has horrible long-term consequences."[72]

Bottom line: get employers out of the health insurance business. To do that, the government mandate for employers to provide health insurance coverage would have to be eliminated, and two changes would need to be made to the U.S. Tax Code. First, it would have to be changed so that employers would no longer be allowed to deduct health insurance premiums. Second, if an employer continued paying for a health insurance plan, the employer's premiums would be added proportionally to each employee's W-2. With no tax benefits for employers and employees, employer-sponsored health insurance plans would no longer serve anyone's interest. But we would need a new and better alternative.

That alternative is an *individual health insurance market*. Yes, we should all buy our own health insurance in a free-market system. Contrary to popular belief, this has never been possible as there has never been a national market for health insurance. Even before the Affordable Care Act, also known as Obamacare, we were not allowed to buy health insurance across state lines. Individuals and employers were only allowed to buy health insurance in the state where they resided and only from the insurance companies their state approved with the coverages it mandated; and each state had its own criteria for what constituted a "good policy." I can see states demanding that insurance companies meet a rigid financial soundness test, but I don't believe they should be mandating specific coverages. Some people want policies with all the bells and whistles and are willing to pay for it, while some are willing to accept less comprehensive coverage in order to pay a lower premium.

With the elimination of employer-sponsored plans and state mandates, we could finally have a true national market for health insurance. A national market would enlarge the size of the risk pool for insurers and reduce costs. Health insurance premiums have been increasing for as long as I can remember, and the cost of the plan my wife and I have with Anthem Blue Cross/Blue Shield increased 35.5% this year. I guess the Affordable Care Act isn't helping to control the escalating cost of health insurance. You should note that when it was first instituted, Anthem took the opportunity to eliminate my former plan, one that suited my needs perfectly, and replaced it with an inferior plan with a higher deductible at the same premium; the premiums have been increasing ever since. Americans are spending too high a percentage of their incomes on health insurance, so it is obvious we need more coverage choices and lower premiums. A free market, capitalistic solution just might be the answer.

Let's look at how the elimination of employer-sponsored plans would financially impact employees and employers. In my proposed plan, employers that currently provide a health insurance plan for their employees would be required to give a pay raise to each employee covered under the plan in the amount of what the employer is currently contributing on their behalf. For the employee, this would increase the amount of income taxes and possibly Social Security and Medicare taxes they would be required to pay. There is a simple solution to this: make the premiums that one pays for health insurance for themselves and their family tax deductible. For the employer, the amount they would have to pay into Social Security and Medicare on behalf of their employees would increase, but that would probably be, at least partially, negated by the reduction in the time and costs to shop for and administer their current group plan.

With any health insurance plan, be it employer-sponsored or individually purchased, one of the more tricky balancing acts is how to cost-effectively mandate "Guaranteed Issue" policies when everyone is not obligated to purchase policies. For insurance to be priced fairly for both the policyholders and the insurance companies, it requires the "law of large numbers." We cannot permit people to "play the system" by being allowed to choose to obtain coverage only when it is needed. The medical community and insurance industry should be able to come up with a responsible, cost effective solution.

Let's also get employers out of the retirement plan business. Again, two changes would need to be made to the U.S. Tax Code. First, it would have to be changed so that employers would no longer be allowed to deduct contributions to employer-sponsored retirement plans. Second, if an employer continued contributing to a retirement plan, the employer's contribution would be added to each employee's W-2. With no tax benefits for employers and employees, employer sponsored retirement plans would become extinct.

Before getting into what I feel would be a better alternative, let's look at one of the big problems with employer-sponsored retirement plans. Defined benefit pension plans have put most states into huge amounts of debt through what are called "unfunded future liabilities." These liabilities were created because most states haven't set aside enough money to cover what they will need to pay their current retirees going forward and their future retirees. And remember, if your state is in debt, so are you because your elected officials can raise your taxes almost at will. The unfunded future liabilities of states is staggering; same for municipalities. Do some research and see how these liabilities are affecting your state.

The large unfunded future liabilities of these plans have been created for a number of reasons. One reason is that they have been based on unsound actuarial assumptions. The assumed rate of return has been too high in relation to what has been and is being earned. This has caused plans to deposit less money each year than what has actually been needed to fund future obligations. Another reason is that some plans have a benefit formula based on an employee's last three years of pay, normally the highest earning years, and they have allowed overtime pay to count in this formula. Some of these employees cram in a boatload of overtime during those last three years and end up with a pension larger than their normal, forty hours per week pay. How does this make sense? Benefit formulas should have been capped at an employee's pay for a forty-hour week and should not have included cost of living increases. Elected officials obligating state residents to such high payments is criminal.

There are other reasons for the pension mess our states are in, but the last one I will address in this pamphlet is the fact that state and municipal governments have continually succumbed to pressure from unions to provide richer and richer benefits. Our elected officials have found it easier to make promises that will help them get re-elected rather than educate the public and make the necessary, difficult, and fiscally sound decisions that our country needs.

Please note that many large corporations have financially sound defined benefit pension plans, although fewer and fewer are offering them to new hires. The major difference between these plans and those run by a state or municipality is in who is responsible for the liability. If a corporation's unfunded liabilities get too large, it is up to the corporation to figure out how to resolve the problem. It only affects employees and shareholders of the corporation and doesn't affect, unlike a state or municipality, *We the People*.

Yes, there are other retirement plans employers can offer, but all are costly to administer, and they don't give employees enough control over investment options. Many of the investment options within 401-K plans have much higher management fees than you would be charged if you invested directly through firms such as Fidelity, Vanguard, and Charles Schwab. Believe me, high administrative and investment management fees are devastating to your portfolio over a long period of time.

I believe a better and less costly retirement plan would be what I call a "Super IRA." In this plan, individuals would be allowed to make a deposit of up to $50,000 per year, and each year this figure would change based on the percentage change in the Consumer Price Index. With the Super IRA, you would have a choice of making a tax-deductible deposit and have all earnings grow tax-deferred, or making your deposit without a tax deduction and have your earnings grow tax-free.

Purchasing and managing benefit programs is very costly for employers, so it limits how many employees they can hire and how much they can pay in wages. Therefore, I believe getting employers out of the "benefits business" would be a boon for employment and wages. But I do see some hurdles to getting my idea passed.

First, I assume the large health insurance companies prefer the status quo and would rather deal with thousands of employers than millions of individuals. However, can you imagine how great it would be to have several insurance companies competing for your business and offering you a variety of policy choices? I see eliminating unnecessary coverages and reduced premiums.

Second, I assume doctors and hospitals also prefer the status quo. They both already have high costs of doing business, including heavy exposure to liability claims, so having to either take the time or hire someone to understand what each policy covers or doesn't cover probably wouldn't be welcome. I would like to think that could be worked out.

Third, I know that unions prefer the status quo. Employee benefit plans are major points of negotiation. Take that away, and union members might want a reduction in their dues. If you ask me, unions only being able to negotiate for fair pay and good, safe working conditions makes a tremendous amount of sense.

Fourth, I know that many of our elected officials prefer the status quo. They have no faith that *We the People* can make wise choices regarding our health insurance and retirement plans. I have more faith than that. In addition, once each individual is in charge of his or her own money, financial and insurance advisory firms will finally be able to afford to provide professional services to the masses. To date, these firms have not been able to do it cost effectively because most people have more assets in their employer's retirement plan than they do in their personal savings and investment accounts, and health insurance is often provided by an employer.

I am not optimistic that the elimination of employee benefit plans will come into existence, but I believe it would benefit the masses.

Chapter 20
Immigration

We are a country built and founded by immigrants. Almost every one of our ancestors came to America in order to create a better life for themselves, their children, their children's children, and even you. The United States has always been considered the land of opportunity, and contrary to some on the Left, it still is. Since we are never going to become complete isolationists, we need an effective immigration policy, not one centered on a wall, but one that helps grow our economy, creates a more prosperous society for all, and one that does strict background checks to assure that suspected terrorists are not allowed in.

The policy we enact must not put a financial burden on our country that would cause our elected officials to want to raise our taxes or put us further into debt. This means not allowing immigrants to be immediately eligible to collect welfare or receive healthcare benefits from a government assistance program. It may sound callous, but to be allowed to immigrate to America, one must be able to make it on his/her own, or they should go back to the country from which they came. With over $19 trillion of debt, we are not in a financial position to support the world.

With around 11.5 million illegal immigrants in our country, we are not going to be able to track them all down. So, the policy we enact should offer those who are here illegally a number of paths to legally work and live in America. On October 30, 2015, Alex Nowrasteh, an immigration policy analyst at the Cato Institute's Center for Global Liberty and Prosperity, wrote in *The Hill* about a three-tiered system that he would like Congress to offer unauthorized immigrants. "The first tier can be very cheap and lead to a permanent renewable work permit. It won't ever allow welfare benefits or family sponsorship, but it will allow the migrant to work legally, own property, get a driver's license, and otherwise participate in American life. The second tier can be a more expensive path to a permanent green card that doesn't need renewal. It can allow partial family sponsorship, deny welfare, but it cannot lead to citizenship for the formerly illegal migrant himself. The third step would lead to citizenship, but it should be the most expensive and difficult: mirroring the Senate's legalization path in its 2013 bill. Most unauthorized immigrants will not choose this path, but the option of citizenship will be open to those who want it most—at a price."[73]

Mr. Nowrasteh did not elaborate on what the prices would be for the three tiers, and I am not overly familiar with the Senate's bill, but the overall strategy seems to make sense and is one that our leaders should explore before putting up a costly wall.

Chapter 21
Abortion

It is beyond my comprehension that every four years, during a presidential election year, abortion becomes a major political topic. Frankly, I don't believe it should be a political issue. I believe it is a personal issue of the parties involved: the mother, first and foremost; the father; and the God, if any, they believe in.

Those who oppose abortion on the political stage claim it is in direct conflict with the Declaration of Independence and our Constitution. They correctly quote the Declaration of Independence, where it is stated that we are all endowed by our Creator with the right to Life, Liberty and the pursuit of Happiness. They correctly point out that the 14th Amendment says we should not be deprived of life, liberty or property, without due process of law. However, to understand what our Founders meant, you must refer to the meaning of the words *abortion*, *life*, *born*, *birth*, *fetus*, *extraction*, and *conception* at the time our country was founded, not today's definitions. Again, the best source is Webster's 1828 Dictionary, and the definitions follow:

"Abortion" was defined as: 1) The act of miscarrying, or producing young before the natural time, or before the fetus is perfectly formed; 2) The fetus brought forth before it is perfectly formed.

"Life" was defined as: The present state of existence; the time from birth to death. The life of a man seldom exceeds seventy years.

"Born" was defined as: To be produced or brought into life.

"Birth" was defined as: The act of coming into life, or of being born; extraction; the act of bringing forth.

"Extraction" was defined as: The act of drawing out; the extraction of a fetus or child in midwifery.

"Fetus" was defined as: The young of viviparous animals in the womb, and of oviparous animals in the egg, after it is perfectly formed; before which time it is called embryo. A young animal then is called a fetus from the time its parts are distinctly formed, till its birth.

"Conception" was defined as: The act of conceiving; the first formation of the embryo or fetus of an animal.

By understanding the definitions of the words used by our Founders, you see that they defined "life" as beginning at "birth," and "birth" was defined as the time a distinctly formed fetus is extracted from the mother. Today, some claim that "conception" is the start of "life." However, in the Declaration of Independence and the Constitution, the Founders never spoke of the word conception and were clear in their definition of life. Therefore, fighting the legality of "abortion" on Constitutional grounds is unfounded.

Apparently, Lee Edwards from the Heritage Foundation needs to pull out Webster's 1828 Dictionary. He wrote in the *Daily Signal* on February 24, 2016 that "American conservatism does not need warmed-over Republicanism from the Fifties," and amongst other things he proposes the "protection of human life from conception to natural death."[74] I always thought he and the Heritage Foundation were proponents of the small government our Founders envisioned and wanted to adhere to the Constitution; guess I was wrong.

Back to where I started: abortion is not a political issue, it is a personal issue. In *Somebody's Gotta Say It*, Neal Boortz argues that "It is possible to dislike abortion and still be pro-choice."[75] He goes on to say, "The terminology is not 'pro-abortion' and 'pro-life.' It's 'pro-choice' and 'anti-choice.'"[76] Interestingly, although Mr. Boortz is personally against abortion, he is more against having a government that oversteps its boundaries with more and more regulations that take away the freedoms our Founders fought so hard to attain.

Should abortions be regulated? Of course. Protecting a mother's rights and health, protecting doctors who perform abortions, and protecting a fully functional, healthy unborn fetus that could be delivered without harming the mother should be taken into consideration with any and all regulations.

I hope never again to hear individuals campaigning for the office of president of the United States be asked by the media to discuss their feelings on abortion or overturning *Roe v. Wade*. Who cares what they think on the subject? It's a personal issue...enough already!

Chapter 22
Gay/Lesbian Rights

Like abortion, this is another topic I no longer want debated. In my opinion, this is another social issue, not one the government should be involved with. Republicans claim to be advocates of less regulation, freedom, and small government. Then why are they always looking to expand the government's regulatory authority in social issues with which government should have no jurisdiction?

I don't believe that homosexuality is a choice; you are either born homosexual or heterosexual, and you can't do anything about it. Therefore, homosexuals should not be discriminated against. To quote Neal Boortz, "If it were a choice, why would one choose a lifestyle where they are discriminated against on the job and in their church, and where they are constantly derided and condemned by much of society? Instead of being a solid and respected member of the community, do you think they chose to opt for a lifestyle where idiots assume that they are child molesters?"[77] The world has come a long way since Mr. Boortz wrote that in 2007, but discrimination still exists.

Michelle Caruso-Cabrera says that "The gay-marriage debate would basically go away if states would just stop giving out marriage licenses—for anyone, straight or gay. Government's role is to defend contracts—not decide who should enter into one. Why does the state get involved with this at all? Why do I have to go to the courthouse if I am also going to go to my church, synagogue, or whatever house of worship to which I belong? There are witnesses you can sign a contract in front of; it will hold up in a court of law later if you want to get divorced. In the end, marriage should be a private contract between two people, regardless of sexual orientation. If gays and lesbians want to marry, they could do it at an institution that welcomes them. Think of it like privatizing marriage. Why is government going to places it shouldn't go? My guess is that it wants the license fees, but that's another issue."[78]

Ms. Caruso-Cabrera goes on to say, "If states didn't issue marriage licenses at all, then states wouldn't have to worry about defining marriage in the first place and then could avoid all the moral meddling that comes along. This would allow various members of state legislatures to focus on the bread-and-butter issues facing American families and stop wasting money advocating for or against a constitutional amendment to define the state of wedlock."[79]

Republicans wonder why they have a hard time winning the popular vote in presidential elections. They need to look no further than their misguided attempts to pontificate on and regulate social matters, despite the lack of a Constitutional right to do so.

Chapter 23
Other Important Issues to Consider

In this chapter, I briefly discuss several important issues that I believe need to be considered by our elected officials.

The human race needs clean air and drinking water to survive. A common sense, economical strategy is needed, not one based on unproven suppositions, nor one that will break the bank as we along with most countries around the world are not without financial concerns. We must set the standard, and then get the other countries to follow our lead because air and water pollution in one country are not containable to that region and affect the whole world.

Relating to clean water, it would be nice if we can figure out a cost-effective way to convert salt water into fresh water, so no one in this world ever has to worry about running out of drinking water.

For years, many people have thought that drug addiction should be looked at as a disease rather than a crime. In May of 2015, Leonard Campanello, the police chief of Gloucester, Massachusetts, took it a step further, and according to a January 24, 2016 article in the *New York Times* by Katherine Seelye, made this announcement: "Any addict who walks into the police station with the remainder of their drug equipment (needles, etc.) or drugs and asks for help will not be charged. Instead we will walk them through the system toward detox and recovery."[80] Ms. Seelye pointed out that although there have been some critics that do not believe a police chief has the authority to do what he did, other police departments from around the country have viewed his "approach as a promising way to address the epidemic of heroin and prescription pain pills, which together killed 47,055 people in 2014 nationwide—more than died in car accidents, homicides or suicides." She also reported that since the program's inception, 391 addicts have turned themselves in to the Gloucester police department, and that fifty-six other police departments in seventeen states have started programs with a similar model.[81]

A related article from *Elite Daily* by Jill Pohl on May 15, 2015 reported that according to the National Institute on Drug Abuse,

"Treatment offers the best alternative for interrupting the drug/ criminal justice cycle for offenders with drug problems. Treatment can help individuals...change attitudes, beliefs and behaviors; avoid relapse; and successfully remove themselves from a life of substance abuse and crime."[82] She also reported that the journal *Crime & Delinquency* found the following: "If just 10 percent of eligible offenders were treated in community-based programs instead of going to prison, the criminal justice system would save $4.8 billion."[83]

With drug abuse on the rise, particularly heroin, it seems like a good time to try the new approach Chief Campanello is advocating.

Another point worth raising is America is in need of campaign finance reform—it just shouldn't cost as much as it does to run for political office. The United States was not supposed to be governed by only rich people. Running for political office needs to become affordable for all Americans. The nation is supposed to be governed by bright individuals who care more about our country than any political party, and that is not what I see today. Let's reverse *Citizens United* and other laws that help only a few control who gets elected.

In *A Declaration of Independents*, Greg Orman sums it up nicely: "Our system of self-government is being compromised by a campaign finance system that allows special interests to buy politicians and elections. The parties have become a duopoly and are behaving like one—dramatically limiting competition and, by extension, limiting accountability." He went on to say that "We are sending the worst of both parties to Washington—bitter partisans who care more about pleasing the extremists and special interests in their own party than they do moving the country forward."[84]

How do you get our elected officials and political parties to compromise and accomplish great things when they are so concerned about getting re-elected that they tell their constituents what they want to hear—not what they need to hear—and placate their donors? Time for a new system.

The Second Amendment gives us the right to bear arms. However, a reasonable person should have no problem with regulations regarding ownership, such as background checks, waiting periods, possibly a mental health test, and the types of arms allowed. Personally, I see no reason why assault weapons shouldn't be banned.

There is often talk about removing the word God from public buildings, U.S. currency, and in the classroom. And some don't want public displays honoring God during religious holidays such a Christmas. Those who feel this way claim that the word *God* shouldn't be used because it is in conflict with the First Amendment. Give me a break! The First Amendment reads: "Congress shall make no law respecting an establishment of religion, or prohibiting the free exercise thereof; or abridging the freedom of speech, or of the press; or the right of the people peaceably to assemble, and to petition the Government for a redress of grievances." God is not even mentioned; religion is. Therefore, our Founders did not say that there needs to be a separation between God and state. And when you read the Declaration of Independence, you will know that there is no separation.

As stated in the Declaration of Independence, our country was founded on the rights God gave all mankind. Given that humans are imperfect, His wishes have not been carried out perfectly. That may be one of the reasons some people are atheists and some are agnostic, and may be the reason why some feel that God should not be honored publicly. Choosing to not believe in God or question God's existence is an individual choice that must be respected. However, there is no reason why we cannot publicly honor the One who gave our Founders the inspiration to form a republic based on His laws and create a constitution that has lasted longer than any in history.

The Supreme Court is authorized by the Constitution of the United States to interpret and rule on laws, not create law; that is up to Congress and each state legislature. It concerns me that the Supreme Court has become so politicized. The judges are supposed to preserve, protect, and defend the Constitution of the United States. They are to interpret for the rest of us what the Founders meant when they created this precious document. Each judge's liberal or conservative personal interpretation of what he or she wishes the Founders were saying is irrelevant; that is not a judge's job. The judges should be going back to the meaning of each word in the Constitution as it was used when it was written, and then speak and rule on the Founders' behalf. It is time to get politics out of the Court!

In reading Article III, Section 1 of the Constitution, it says that "The Judges, both of the supreme and inferior Courts, shall hold their

Offices during good Behaviour, and shall, at stated Times, receive for their Services a Compensation which shall not be diminished during their Continuance in Office." I do not interpret that to mean a life-long appointment, but I could be wrong. I wonder what our Founders *really* meant.

I have to admit, I never envisioned public bathrooms being a much talked about social issue. Now that it is, I will add my two cents, for what it is worth. I believe that allowing people to use the public bathroom of the sex they most identity with rather than the one they were born with leaves too much room for abuse. I feel there are two options:

1. Require people to use the public bathroom that fits the sexual parts they possess. In other words, if you have a penis, you shouldn't use the lady's room.

2. Create a third set of bathrooms that are unisex.

Lastly, we are more humane to animals than we are to humans. When an animal is too sick to recover, the veterinarian suggests that the animal be put down. Why do humans force other humans to suffer? Just asking!

Chapter 24
Conclusion

I hope my vision of a more fiscally responsible, socially accepting nation resonates with you. I believe about 60% to 80% of Americans believe the way I do; therefore, we need to figure out a way to not let the ideological far Left and far Right dominate political agendas and primaries, so that we can end up with good candidates from each party who truly represent the majority of Americans.

Our country cannot continue with: uncontrolled spending and borrowing; running up huge debt that will negatively impact future generations; leaving individuals and businesses in a climate of tax and regulatory uncertainty; subjecting our youth, particularly those in the inner cities, to an inferior educational system; and drifting away from our Founders' principles toward the failed social democracies of Europe where they have promised their citizens more than they can afford.

Our country must become more accepting of others, no matter the color of their skin, religious beliefs, political beliefs, or sexual orientation. Let's all get along!

Our elected officials need to realize that they work for us; we do not work for them. They need to realize that *We the People* can handle the truth about our country's finances. Thomas Sowell writes, "When you want to help people, you tell them the truth. When you want to help yourself, you tell them what they want to hear."[85] It is time for our elected officials in Washington to come clean, to take the time and energy to be honest and educate us with one set of unified facts, and stop being so concerned with getting re-elected.

When you include the interest payment on our national debt, mandatory spending, also known as "entitlement programs," is roughly 70 percent of our country's annual budget. With such a high percentage, we can't possibly fix our nation's financial troubles without addressing the cost of these programs; and we better do it quickly. As Ken Langone, one of the founders of Home Depot (and in my opinion, one of the most pragmatic individuals in the world), said when he was recently interviewed on CNBC, "The fact of the matter is, the grim reaper is coming," and that we need "elected officials [with] the political courage to do what's right as opposed to do what's good for him to get reelected."[86] With our aging population, mandatory spending will continue to become a larger portion of our budget if left unchecked, so it is time to act.

Our elected officials also do not need to micromanage our personal lives. In *The Right Path*, Joe Scarborough shares a quote from President Ronald Reagan about a government that gets too large and oversteps its authority: "This is the issue of this election: Whether we believe in our capacity for self-government or whether we abandon the American Revolution and confess that a little, intellectual elite in a far-distant capital can plan our lives for us better than we can plan them for ourselves."[87] Ronald Reagan had faith in *We the People*; I have faith in *We the People*. I hope you do, too.

Although I am a proponent of the small, limited government that our Founders advocated, there are, of course, times when our federal government should intercede. In *The Road to Freedom*, Arthur Brooks also states that there are indeed times when the federal government should step in and intervene in the private market, and he has created the flow chart below to determine when it is appropriate.[88]

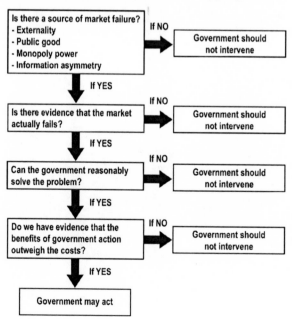

Dr. Brooks' chart makes sense to me!

Greg Orman sums up what voters are looking for: "They want elected officials who tell the truth, even if that means relaying harsh facts. They want elected officials with the courage to stand up to the special interests that control fundraising apparatuses in both parties. They want elected officials who don't go to Washington to enrich themselves personally or who view public office as a lifelong career. They want elected officials who care about this country's future— not in the lip-service way, but in the way that makes them willing to make hard choices and encourage fellow Americans to do likewise. They want citizen politicians to serve as actual public servants. They want real leaders."[89] I hope you feel the same, and I encourage you to take the time to learn as much as possible about those running for public office. Making informed decisions is good for your pocketbook because what these elected officials spend on government programs is not their money, it is yours.

A more peaceful, prosperous nation is only possible if we are a unified nation. As Abraham Lincoln famously said, "A house divided against itself cannot stand." He was absolutely right. I hope you are as interested as I am in attaining Mr. Lincoln's goal.

Our best path to a unified nation: electing government officials who put our country first and have an approach that is fiscally responsible and socially accepting—the Centrist approach.

The Declaration of Independence

In Congress, July 4, 1776.

The unanimous Declaration of the thirteen United States of America, When in the Course of human events, it becomes necessary for one people to dissolve the political bands which have connected them with another, and to assume among the powers of the earth, the separate and equal station to which the Laws of Nature and of Nature's God entitle them, a decent respect to the opinions of mankind requires that they should declare the causes which impel them to the separation.

We hold these truths to be self-evident, that all men are created equal, that they are endowed by their Creator with certain unalienable Rights, that among these are Life, Liberty and the pursuit of Happiness.--That to secure these rights, Governments are instituted among Men, deriving their just powers from the consent of the governed, --That whenever any Form of Government becomes destructive of these ends, it is the Right of the People to alter or to abolish it, and to institute new Government, laying its foundation on such principles and organizing its powers in such form, as to them shall seem most likely to affect their Safety and Happiness. Prudence, indeed, will dictate that Governments long established should not be changed for light and transient causes; and accordingly all experience hath shewn, that mankind are more disposed to suffer, while evils are sufferable, than to right themselves by abolishing the forms to which they are accustomed. But when a long train of abuses and usurpations, pursuing invariably the same Object evinces a design to reduce them under absolute Despotism, it is their right, it is their duty, to throw off such Government, and to provide new Guards for their future security.--Such has been the patient sufferance of these Colonies; and such is now the necessity which constrains them to alter their former Systems of Government. The history of the present King of Great Britain is a history of repeated injuries and usurpations, all having in direct object the establishment of an absolute Tyranny over these States. To prove this, let Facts be submitted to a candid world.

He has refused his Assent to Laws, the most wholesome and necessary for the public good.

He has forbidden his Governors to pass Laws of immediate and pressing importance, unless suspended in their operation till his Assent should be obtained; and when so suspended, he has utterly neglected to attend to them.

He has refused to pass other Laws for the accommodation of large districts of people, unless those people would relinquish the right of Representation in the Legislature, a right inestimable to them and formidable to tyrants only.

He has called together legislative bodies at places unusual, uncomfortable, and distant from the depository of their public Records, for the sole purpose of fatiguing them into compliance with his measures.

He has dissolved Representative Houses repeatedly, for opposing with manly firmness his invasions on the rights of the people.

He has refused for a long time, after such dissolutions, to cause others to be elected; whereby the Legislative powers, incapable of Annihilation, have returned to the People at large for their exercise; the State remaining in the meantime exposed to all the dangers of invasion from without, and convulsions within.

He has endeavoured to prevent the population of these States; for that purpose obstructing the Laws for Naturalization of Foreigners; refusing to pass others to encourage their migrations hither, and raising the conditions of new Appropriations of Lands.

He has obstructed the Administration of Justice, by refusing his Assent to Laws for establishing Judiciary powers.

He has made Judges dependent on his Will alone, for the tenure of their offices, and the amount and payment of their salaries.

He has erected a multitude of New Offices, and sent hither swarms of Officers to harrass our people, and eat out their substance.

He has kept among us, in times of peace, Standing Armies without the Consent of our legislatures.

He has affected to render the Military independent of and superior to the Civil power.

He has combined with others to subject us to a jurisdiction foreign to our constitution, and unacknowledged by our laws; giving his Assent to their Acts of pretended Legislation:

For Quartering large bodies of armed troops among us:

For protecting them, by a mock Trial, from punishment for any Murders which they should commit on the Inhabitants of these States:

For cutting off our Trade with all parts of the world:

For imposing Taxes on us without our Consent:

For depriving us in many cases, of the benefits of Trial by Jury:

For transporting us beyond Seas to be tried for pretended offences

For abolishing the free System of English Laws in a neighbouring Province, establishing therein an Arbitrary government, and enlarging its Boundaries so as to render it at once an example and fit instrument for introducing the same absolute rule into these Colonies:

For taking away our Charters, abolishing our most valuable Laws, and altering fundamentally the Forms of our Governments:

For suspending our own Legislatures, and declaring themselves invested with power to legislate for us in all cases whatsoever.

He has abdicated Government here, by declaring us out of his Protection and waging War against us.

He has plundered our seas, ravaged our Coasts, burnt our towns, and destroyed the lives of our people.

He is at this time transporting large Armies of foreign Mercenaries to compleat the works of death, desolation and tyranny, already begun with circumstances of Cruelty & perfidy scarcely paralleled in the most barbarous ages, and totally unworthy the Head of a civilized nation.

He has constrained our fellow Citizens taken Captive on the high Seas to bear Arms against their Country, to become the executioners of their friends and Brethren, or to fall themselves by their Hands.

He has excited domestic insurrections amongst us, and has endeavoured to bring on the inhabitants of our frontiers, the merciless Indian Savages, whose known rule of warfare, is an undistinguished destruction of all ages, sexes and conditions.

In every stage of these Oppressions We have Petitioned for Redress in the most humble terms: Our repeated Petitions have been answered only by repeated injury. A Prince whose character is thus marked by every act which may define a Tyrant, is unfit to be the ruler of a free people.

Nor have We been wanting in attentions to our British brethren. We have warned them from time to time of attempts by their legislature to extend an unwarrantable jurisdiction over us. We have reminded them of the circumstances of our emigration and settlement here. We have appealed to their native justice and magnanimity, and we have conjured them by the ties of our common kindred to disavow these usurpations, which, would inevitably interrupt our connections and correspondence. They too have been deaf to the voice of justice and of consanguinity. We must, therefore, acquiesce in the necessity, which denounces our Separation, and hold them, as we hold the rest of mankind, Enemies in War, in Peace Friends.

We, therefore, the Representatives of the united States of America, in General Congress, Assembled, appealing to the Supreme Judge of the world for the rectitude of our intentions, do, in the Name, and by Authority of the good People of these Colonies, solemnly publish and declare, That these United Colonies are, and of Right ought to be Free and Independent States; that they are Absolved from all Allegiance to the British Crown, and that all political connection between them and the State of Great Britain, is and ought to be totally dissolved; and that as Free and Independent States, they have full Power to levy War, conclude Peace, contract Alliances, establish Commerce, and to do all other Acts and Things which Independent States may of right do. And for the support of this Declaration, with a firm reliance on the protection of divine Providence, we mutually pledge to each other our Lives, our Fortunes and our sacred Honor.

Georgia
Button Gwinnett
Lyman Hall
George Walton

North Carolina
William Hooper
Joseph Hewes
John Penn

South Carolina
Edward Rutledge
Thomas Heyward, Jr.
Thomas Lynch, Jr.
Arthur Middleton

Massachusetts
John Hancock

Maryland
Samuel Chase
William Paca
Thomas Stone
Charles Carroll of
Carrollton

Virginia
George Wythe
Richard Henry Lee
Thomas Jefferson
Benjamin Harrison
Thomas Nelson, Jr.
Francis Lightfoot Lee
Carter Braxton

Pennsylvania
Robert Morris
Benjamin Rush
Benjamin Franklin
John Morton
George Clymer
James Smith
George Taylor
James Wilson
George Ross

Delaware
Caesar Rodney
George Read
Thomas McKean

New York
William Floyd
Philip Livingston
Francis Lewis
Lewis Morris

New Jersey
Richard Stockton
John Witherspoon
Francis Hopkinson
John Hart
Abraham Clark

New Hampshire
Josiah Bartlett
William Whipple
Matthew Thornton

Massachusetts
Samuel Adams
John Adams
Robert Treat Paine
Elbridge Gerry

Rhode Island
Stephen Hopkins
William Ellery

Connecticut
Roger Sherman
Samuel Huntington
William Williams
Oliver Wolcott

The Constitution of the United States of America

(Note that the italicized words in the Constitution were later amended or suspended.)

We the People of the United States, in Order to form a more perfect Union, establish Justice, insure domestic Tranquility, provide for the common defence, promote the general Welfare, and secure the Blessings of Liberty to ourselves and our Posterity, do ordain and establish this Constitution for the United States of America.

Article. I.

Section. 1.

All legislative Powers herein granted shall be vested in a Congress of the United States, which shall consist of a Senate and House of Representatives.

Section. 2.

The House of Representatives shall be composed of Members chosen every second Year by the People of the several States, and the Electors in each State shall have the Qualifications requisite for Electors of the most numerous Branch of the State Legislature.

No Person shall be a Representative who shall not have attained to the Age of twenty-five Years, and been seven Years a Citizen of the United States, and who shall not, when elected, be an Inhabitant of that State in which he shall be chosen.

Representatives and direct Taxes shall be apportioned among the several States which may be included within this Union, according to their respective Numbers, which shall be determined by adding to the whole Number of free Persons, including those bound to Service for a Term of Years, and excluding Indians not taxed, three fifths of all other Persons. The actual Enumeration shall be made within three Years after the first Meeting of the Congress of the United States, and within every subsequent Term of ten Years, in such Manner as they shall by Law direct. The Number of Representatives shall not exceed one for every thirty Thousand, but each State shall have at Least one Representative; and until such enumeration shall be made, the State of New Hampshire shall be entitled to chuse three, Massachusetts eight, Rhode-Island and Providence Plantations one, Connecticut five, New-York six, New Jersey four, Pennsylvania eight, Delaware one, Maryland six, Virginia ten, North Carolina five, South Carolina five, and Georgia three.

When vacancies happen in the Representation from any State, the Executive Authority thereof shall issue Writs of Election to fill such Vacancies.

The House of Representatives shall chuse their Speaker and other Officers; and shall have the sole Power of Impeachment.

Section. 3.

The Senate of the United States shall be composed of two Senators from each State, *chosen by the Legislature thereof,* for six Years; and each Senator shall have one Vote.

Immediately after they shall be assembled in Consequence of the first Election, they shall be divided as equally as may be into three Classes. The Seats of the Senators of the first Class shall be vacated at the Expiration of the second Year, of the second Class at the Expiration of the fourth Year, and of the third Class at the Expiration of the sixth Year, so that one third may be chosen every second Year; *and if Vacancies happen by Resignation, or otherwise, during the Recess of the Legislature of any State, the Executive thereof may make temporary Appointments until the next Meeting of the Legislature, which shall then fill such Vacancies.*

No Person shall be a Senator who shall not have attained to the Age of thirty Years, and been nine Years a Citizen of the United States, and who shall not, when elected, be an Inhabitant of that State for which he shall be chosen.

The Vice President of the United States shall be President of the Senate, but shall have no Vote, unless they be equally divided.

The Senate shall chuse their other Officers, and also a President pro tempore, in the Absence of the Vice President, or when he shall exercise the Office of President of the United States.

The Senate shall have the sole Power to try all Impeachments. When sitting for that Purpose, they shall be on Oath or Affirmation. When the President of the United States is tried, the Chief Justice shall preside: And no Person shall be convicted without the Concurrence of two thirds of the Members present.

Judgment in Cases of Impeachment shall not extend further than to removal from Office, and disqualification to hold and enjoy any Office of honor, Trust or Profit under the United States: but the Party convicted shall nevertheless be liable and subject to Indictment, Trial, Judgment and Punishment, according to Law.

Section. 4.

The Times, Places and Manner of holding Elections for Senators and Representatives, shall be prescribed in each State by the Legislature thereof; but the Congress may at any time by Law make or alter such Regulations, except as to the Places of chusing Senators.

The Congress shall assemble at least once in every Year, and such Meeting shall be on *the first Monday in December*, unless they shall by Law appoint a different Day.

Section. 5.

Each House shall be the Judge of the Elections, Returns and Qualifications of its own Members, and a Majority of each shall constitute a Quorum to do Business; but a smaller Number may adjourn from day to day, and may be authorized to compel the Attendance of absent Members, in such Manner, and under such Penalties as each House may provide.

Each House may determine the Rules of its Proceedings, punish its Members for disorderly Behaviour, and, with the Concurrence of two thirds, expel a Member.

Each House shall keep a Journal of its Proceedings, and from time to time publish the same, excepting such Parts as may in their Judgment require Secrecy; and the Yeas and Nays of the Members of either House on any question shall, at the Desire of one fifth of those Present, be entered on the Journal.

Neither House, during the Session of Congress, shall, without the Consent of the other, adjourn for more than three days, nor to any other Place than that in which the two Houses shall be sitting.

Section. 6.

The Senators and Representatives shall receive a Compensation for their Services, to be ascertained by Law, and paid out of the Treasury of the United States. They shall in all Cases, except Treason, Felony and Breach of the Peace, be privileged from Arrest during their Attendance at the Session of their respective Houses, and in going to and returning from the same; and for any Speech or Debate in either House, they shall not be questioned in any other Place.

No Senator or Representative shall, during the Time for which he was elected, be appointed to any civil Office under the Authority of the United States, which shall have been created, or the Emoluments whereof shall have been encreased during such time; and no Person holding any Office under the United States, shall be a Member of either House during his Continuance in Office.

Section. 7.

All Bills for raising Revenue shall originate in the House of Representatives; but the Senate may propose or concur with Amendments as on other Bills.

Every Bill which shall have passed the House of Representatives and the Senate, shall, before it become a Law, be presented to the President of the United States; If he approves he shall sign it, but if not he shall return it, with his Objections to that House in which it shall have originated, who shall enter the Objections at large on their Journal, and proceed to reconsider it. If after such Reconsideration two thirds of that House shall agree to pass the Bill, it shall be sent, together with the Objections, to the other House, by which it shall likewise be reconsidered, and if approved by two thirds of that House, it shall become a Law. But in all such Cases the Votes of both Houses shall be determined by yeas and Nays, and the Names of the Persons voting for and against the Bill shall be entered on the Journal of each House respectively. If any Bill shall not be returned by the President within ten Days (Sundays excepted) after it shall have been presented to him, the Same shall be a Law, in like Manner as if he had signed it, unless the Congress by their Adjournment prevent its Return, in which Case it shall not be a Law.

Every Order, Resolution, or Vote to which the Concurrence of the Senate and House of Representatives may be necessary (except on a question of Adjournment) shall be presented to the President of the United States; and before the Same shall take Effect, shall be approved by him, or being disapproved by him, shall be repassed by two thirds of the Senate and House of Representatives, according to the Rules and Limitations prescribed in the Case of a Bill.

Section. 8.

The Congress shall have Power To lay and collect Taxes, Duties, Imposts and Excises, to pay the Debts and provide for the common Defence and general Welfare of the United States; but all Duties, Imposts and Excises shall be uniform throughout the United States;

To borrow Money on the credit of the United States;

To regulate Commerce with foreign Nations, and among the several States, and with the Indian Tribes;

To establish an uniform Rule of Naturalization, and uniform Laws on the subject of Bankruptcies throughout the United States;

To coin Money, regulate the Value thereof, and of foreign Coin, and fix the Standard of Weights and Measures;

To provide for the Punishment of counterfeiting the Securities and current Coin of the United States;

To establish Post Offices and post Roads;

To promote the Progress of Science and useful Arts, by securing for limited Times to Authors and Inventors the exclusive Right to their respective Writings and Discoveries;

To constitute Tribunals inferior to the supreme Court;

To define and punish Piracies and Felonies committed on the high Seas, and Offences against the Law of Nations;

To declare War, grant Letters of Marque and Reprisal, and make Rules concerning Captures on Land and Water;

To raise and support Armies, but no Appropriation of Money to that Use shall be for a longer Term than two Years;

To provide and maintain a Navy;

To make Rules for the Government and Regulation of the land and naval Forces;

To provide for calling forth the Militia to execute the Laws of the Union, suppress Insurrections and repel Invasions;

To provide for organizing, arming, and disciplining, the Militia, and for governing such Part of them as may be employed in the Service of the United States, reserving to the States respectively, the Appointment of the Officers, and the Authority of training the Militia according to the discipline prescribed by Congress;

To exercise exclusive Legislation in all Cases whatsoever, over such District (not exceeding ten Miles square) as may, by Cession of particular States, and the Acceptance of Congress, become the Seat of the Government of the United States, and to exercise like Authority over all Places purchased by the Consent of the Legislature of the State in which the Same shall be, for the Erection of Forts, Magazines, Arsenals, dock-Yards, and other needful Buildings;—And

To make all Laws which shall be necessary and proper for carrying into Execution the foregoing Powers, and all other Powers vested by this Constitution in the Government of the United States, or in any Department or Officer thereof.

Section. 9.

The Migration or Importation of such Persons as any of the States now existing shall think proper to admit, shall not be prohibited by the Congress prior to the Year one thousand eight hundred and eight, but a Tax or duty may be imposed on such Importation, not exceeding ten dollars for each Person.

The Privilege of the Writ of Habeas Corpus shall not be suspended, unless when in Cases of Rebellion or Invasion the public Safety may require it.

No Bill of Attainder or ex post facto Law shall be passed.

No Capitation, or other direct, Tax shall be laid, *unless in Proportion to the Census or enumeration herein before directed to be taken*.

No Tax or Duty shall be laid on Articles exported from any State.

No Preference shall be given by any Regulation of Commerce or Revenue to the Ports of one State over those of another: nor shall Vessels bound to, or from, one State, be obliged to enter, clear, or pay Duties in another.

No Money shall be drawn from the Treasury, but in Consequence of Appropriations made by Law; and a regular Statement and Account of the Receipts and Expenditures of all public Money shall be published from time to time.

No Title of Nobility shall be granted by the United States: And no Person holding any Office of Profit or Trust under them, shall, without the Consent of the Congress, accept of any present, Emolument, Office, or Title, of any kind whatever, from any King, Prince, or foreign State.

Section. 10.

No State shall enter into any Treaty, Alliance, or Confederation; grant Letters of Marque and Reprisal; coin Money; emit Bills of Credit; make any Thing but gold and silver Coin a Tender in Payment of Debts; pass any Bill of Attainder, ex post facto Law, or Law impairing the Obligation of Contracts, or grant any Title of Nobility.

No State shall, without the Consent of the Congress, lay any Imposts or Duties on Imports or Exports, except what may be absolutely necessary for executing its inspection Laws: and the net Produce of all Duties and Imposts, laid by any State on Imports or Exports, shall be for the Use of the Treasury of the United States; and all such Laws shall be subject to the Revision and Controul of the Congress.

No State shall, without the Consent of Congress, lay any Duty of Tonnage, keep Troops, or Ships of War in time of Peace, enter into any Agreement or Compact with another State, or with a foreign Power, or engage in War, unless actually invaded, or in such imminent Danger as will not admit of delay.

Article. II.

Section. 1.

The executive Power shall be vested in a President of the United States of America. He shall hold his Office during the Term of four Years, and, together with the Vice President, chosen for the same Term, be elected, as follows:

Each State shall appoint, in such Manner as the Legislature thereof may direct, a Number of Electors, equal to the whole Number of Senators and Representatives to which the State may be entitled in the Congress: but no Senator or Representative, or Person holding an Office of Trust or Profit under the United States, shall be appointed an Elector.

The Electors shall meet in their respective States, and vote by Ballot for two Persons, of whom one at least shall not be an Inhabitant of the same State with themselves. And they shall make a List of all the Persons voted for, and of the Number of Votes for each; which List they shall sign and certify, and transmit sealed to the Seat of the Government of the United States, directed to the President of the Senate. The President of the Senate shall, in the Presence of the Senate and House of Representatives, open all the Certificates, and the Votes shall then be counted. The Person having the greatest Number of Votes shall be the President, if such Number be a Majority of the whole Number of Electors appointed; and if there be more than one who have such Majority, and have an equal Number of Votes, then the House of Representatives shall immediately chuse by Ballot one of them for President; and if no Person have a Majority, then from the five highest on the List the said House shall in like Manner chuse the President. But in chusing the President, the Votes shall be taken by States, the Representation from each State having one Vote; A quorum for this Purpose shall consist of a Member or Members from two thirds of the States, and a Majority of all the States shall be necessary to a Choice. In every Case, after the Choice of the President, the Person having the greatest Number of Votes of the Electors shall be the Vice President. But if there should remain two or more who have equal Votes, the Senate shall chuse from them by Ballot the Vice President.

The Congress may determine the Time of chusing the Electors, and the Day on which they shall give their Votes; which Day shall be the same throughout the United States.

No Person except a natural born Citizen, or a Citizen of the United States, at the time of the Adoption of this Constitution, shall be eligible to the Office of President; neither shall any Person be eligible to that Office who shall not have attained to the Age of thirty five Years, and been fourteen Years a Resident within the United States.

In Case of the Removal of the President from Office, or of his Death, Resignation, or Inability to discharge the Powers and Duties of the said Office, the Same shall devolve on the Vice President, and the Congress may by Law provide for the Case of Removal, Death, Resignation or Inability, both of the President and Vice President, declaring what Officer shall then act as President, and such Officer shall act accordingly, until the Disability be removed, or a President shall be elected.

The President shall, at stated Times, receive for his Services, a Compensation, which shall neither be encreased nor diminished during the Period for which he shall have been elected, and he shall not receive within that Period any other Emolument from the United States, or any of them.

Before he enter on the Execution of his Office, he shall take the following Oath or Affirmation:—"I do solemnly swear (or affirm) that I will faithfully execute the Office of President of the United States, and will to the best of my Ability, preserve, protect and defend the Constitution of the United States."

Section. 2.

The President shall be Commander in Chief of the Army and Navy of the United States, and of the Militia of the several States, when called into the actual Service of the United States; he may require the Opinion, in writing, of the principal Officer in each of the executive Departments, upon any Subject relating to the Duties of their respective Offices, and he shall have Power to grant Reprieves and Pardons for Offences against the United States, except in Cases of Impeachment.

He shall have Power, by and with the Advice and Consent of the Senate, to make Treaties, provided two thirds of the Senators present concur; and he shall nominate, and by and with the Advice and Consent of the Senate, shall appoint Ambassadors, other public Ministers and Consuls, Judges of the supreme Court, and all other Officers of the United States, whose Appointments are not herein otherwise provided for, and which shall be established by Law: but the Congress may by Law vest the Appointment of such inferior Officers, as they think proper, in the President alone, in the Courts of Law, or in the Heads of Departments.

The President shall have Power to fill up all Vacancies that may happen during the Recess of the Senate, by granting Commissions which shall expire at the End of their next Session.

Section. 3.

He shall from time to time give to the Congress Information of the State of the Union, and recommend to their Consideration such Measures as he shall judge necessary and expedient; he may, on extraordinary Occasions, convene both Houses, or either of them, and in Case of Disagreement between them, with Respect to the Time of Adjournment, he may adjourn them to such Time as he shall think proper; he shall receive Ambassadors and other public Ministers; he shall take Care that the Laws be faithfully executed, and shall Commission all the Officers of the United States.

Section. 4.

The President, Vice President and all civil Officers of the United States, shall be removed from Office on Impeachment for, and Conviction of, Treason, Bribery, or other high Crimes and Misdemeanors.

Article. III.

Section. 1.

The judicial Power of the United States, shall be vested in one supreme Court, and in such inferior Courts as the Congress may from time to time ordain and establish. The Judges, both of the supreme and inferior Courts, shall hold their Offices during good Behaviour, and shall, at stated Times, receive for their Services, a Compensation, which shall not be diminished during their Continuance in Office.

Section. 2.

The judicial Power shall extend to all Cases, in Law and Equity, arising under this Constitution, the Laws of the United States, and Treaties made, or which shall be made, under their Authority;—to all Cases affecting Ambassadors, other public Ministers and Consuls;—to all Cases of admiralty and maritime Jurisdiction;—to Controversies to which the United States shall be a Party;—to Controversies between two or more States;—*between a State and Citizens of another State,*—between Citizens of different States,—between Citizens of the same State claiming Lands under Grants of different States, *and between a State, or the Citizens thereof, and foreign States, Citizens or Subjects.*

In all Cases affecting Ambassadors, other public Ministers and Consuls, and those in which a State shall be Party, the supreme Court shall have original Jurisdiction. In all the other Cases before mentioned, the supreme Court shall have appellate Jurisdiction, both as to Law and Fact, with such Exceptions, and under such Regulations as the Congress shall make.

The Trial of all Crimes, except in Cases of Impeachment, shall be by Jury; and such Trial shall be held in the State where the said Crimes shall have been committed; but when not committed within any State, the Trial shall be at such Place or Places as the Congress may by Law have directed.

Section. 3.

Treason against the United States, shall consist only in levying War against them, or in adhering to their Enemies, giving them Aid and Comfort. No Person shall be convicted of Treason unless on the Testimony of two Witnesses to the same overt Act, or on Confession in open Court.

The Congress shall have Power to declare the Punishment of Treason, but no Attainder of Treason shall work Corruption of Blood, or Forfeiture except during the Life of the Person attainted.

Article. IV.

Section. 1.

Full Faith and Credit shall be given in each State to the public Acts, Records, and judicial Proceedings of every other State. And the Congress may by general Laws prescribe the Manner in which such Acts, Records and Proceedings shall be proved, and the Effect thereof.

Section. 2.

The Citizens of each State shall be entitled to all Privileges and Immunities of Citizens in the several States.

A Person charged in any State with Treason, Felony, or other Crime, who shall flee from Justice, and be found in another State, shall on Demand of the executive Authority of the State from which he fled, be delivered up, to be removed to the State having Jurisdiction of the Crime.

No Person held to Service or Labour in one State, under the Laws thereof, escaping into another, shall, in Consequence of any Law or

Regulation therein, be discharged from such Service or Labour, but shall be delivered up on Claim of the Party to whom such Service or Labour may be due.

Section. 3.

New States may be admitted by the Congress into this Union; but no new State shall be formed or erected within the Jurisdiction of any other State; nor any State be formed by the Junction of two or more States, or Parts of States, without the Consent of the Legislatures of the States concerned as well as of the Congress.

The Congress shall have Power to dispose of and make all needful Rules and Regulations respecting the Territory or other Property belonging to the United States; and nothing in this Constitution shall be so construed as to Prejudice any Claims of the United States, or of any particular State.

Section. 4.

The United States shall guarantee to every State in this Union a Republican Form of Government, and shall protect each of them against Invasion; and on Application of the Legislature, or of the Executive (when the Legislature cannot be convened), against domestic Violence.

Article. V.

The Congress, whenever two thirds of both Houses shall deem it necessary, shall propose Amendments to this Constitution, or, on the Application of the Legislatures of two thirds of the several States, shall call a Convention for proposing Amendments, which, in either Case, shall be valid to all Intents and Purposes, as Part of this Constitution, when ratified by the Legislatures of three fourths of the several States, or by Conventions in three fourths thereof, as the one or the other Mode of Ratification may be proposed by the Congress; Provided that no Amendment which may be made prior to the Year One thousand eight hundred and eight shall in any Manner affect the first and fourth Clauses in the Ninth Section of the first Article; and that no State, without its Consent, shall be deprived of its equal Suffrage in the Senate.

Article. VI.

All Debts contracted and Engagements entered into, before the Adoption of this Constitution, shall be as valid against the United States under this Constitution, as under the Confederation.

This Constitution, and the Laws of the United States which shall be made in Pursuance thereof; and all Treaties made, or which shall be made, under the Authority of the United States, shall be the supreme Law of the Land; and the Judges in every State shall be bound thereby, any Thing in the Constitution or Laws of any State to the Contrary notwithstanding.

The Senators and Representatives before mentioned, and the Members of the several State Legislatures, and all executive and judicial Officers, both of the United States and of the several States, shall be bound by Oath or Affirmation, to support this Constitution; but no religious Test shall ever be required as a Qualification to any Office or public Trust under the United States.

Article. VII.

The Ratification of the Conventions of nine States, shall be sufficient for the Establishment of this Constitution between the States so ratifying the Same.

Done in Convention by the Unanimous Consent of the States present the Seventeenth Day of September in the Year of our Lord one thousand seven hundred and Eighty-seven and of the Independance of the United States of America the Twelfth In witness whereof We have hereunto subscribed our Names,

G°. Washington---
President and deputy from Virginia

Delaware
Geo: Read
Gunning Bedford jun
John Dickinson
Richard Bassett
Jaco: Broom

Maryland
James McHenry
Dan of St Thos. Jenifer
Danl. Carroll

Virginia
John Blair
James Madison Jr.

North Carolina
Wm. Blount
Richd. Dobbs Spaight
Hu Williamson

South Carolina
J. Rutledge
Charles Cotesworth Pinckney
Charles Pinckney
Pierce Butler

Georgia
William Few
Abr Baldwin

New Hampshire
John Langdon
Nicholas Gilman

Massachusetts
Nathanial Gorham
Rufus King

Connecticut
Wm. Saml. Johnson
Roger Sherman

New York
Alexander Hamilton

New Jersey
Wil: Livingston
David Brearley
Wm. Paterson
Jona: Dayton

Pennsylvania
B Franklin
Thomas Mifflin
Robt. Morris
Geo. Clymer
Thos. FitzSimmons
Jared Ingersoll
James Wilson
Gouv Morris

Amendments to the Constitution of the United States of America

(The first ten amendments, also known as the Bill of Rights, were ratified on December 15, 1791)

Amendment I

Congress shall make no law respecting an establishment of religion, or prohibiting the free exercise thereof; or abridging the freedom of speech, or of the press; or the right of the people peaceably to assemble, and to petition the Government for a redress of grievances.

Amendment II

A well regulated Militia, being necessary to the security of a free State, the right of the people to keep and bear Arms, shall not be infringed.

Amendment III

No Soldier shall, in time of peace be quartered in any house, without the consent of the Owner, nor in time of war, but in a manner to be prescribed by law.

Amendment IV

The right of the people to be secure in their persons, houses, papers, and effects, against unreasonable searches and seizures, shall not be violated, and no Warrants shall issue, but upon probable cause, supported by Oath or affirmation, and particularly describing the place to be searched, and the persons or things to be seized.

Amendment V

No person shall be held to answer for a capital, or otherwise infamous crime, unless on a presentment or indictment of a Grand Jury, except in cases arising in the land or naval forces, or in the Militia, when in actual service in time of War or public danger; nor shall any person be subject for the same offence to be twice put in jeopardy of life or limb; nor shall be compelled in any criminal case to be a witness against himself, nor be deprived of life, liberty, or property, without due process of law; nor shall private property be taken for public use, without just compensation.

Amendment VI

In all criminal prosecutions, the accused shall enjoy the right to a speedy and public trial, by an impartial jury of the State and district wherein the crime shall have been committed, which district shall have been previously ascertained by law, and to be informed of the nature and cause of the accusation; to be confronted with the witnesses against him; to have compulsory process for obtaining witnesses in his favor, and to have the Assistance of Counsel for his defence.

Amendment VII

In Suits at common law, where the value in controversy shall exceed twenty dollars, the right of trial by jury shall be preserved, and no fact tried by a jury, shall be otherwise re-examined in any Court of the United States, than according to the rules of the common law.

Amendment VIII

Excessive bail shall not be required, nor excessive fines imposed, nor cruel and unusual punishments inflicted.

Amendment IX

The enumeration in the Constitution, of certain rights, shall not be construed to deny or disparage others retained by the people.

Amendment X

The powers not delegated to the United States by the Constitution, nor prohibited by it to the States, are reserved to the States respectively, or to the people.

Amendment XI

Passed by Congress March 4, 1794. Ratified February 7, 1795. Note: Article III, section 2, of the Constitution was modified by amendment 11.

The Judicial power of the United States shall not be construed to extend to any suit in law or equity, commenced or prosecuted against one of the United States by Citizens of another State, or by Citizens or Subjects of any Foreign State.

Amendment XII

Passed by Congress December 9, 1803. Ratified June 15, 1804. Note: A portion of Article II, section 1 of the Constitution was superseded by the 12th amendment.

The Electors shall meet in their respective states and vote by ballot for President and Vice-President, one of whom, at least, shall not be an inhabitant of the same state with themselves; they shall name in their ballots the person voted for as President, and in distinct ballots the person voted for as Vice-President, and they shall make distinct lists of all persons voted for as President, and of all persons voted for as Vice-President, and of the number of votes for each, which lists they shall sign and certify, and transmit sealed to the seat of the government of the United States, directed to the President of the Senate; -- the President of the Senate shall, in the presence of the Senate and House of Representatives, open all the certificates and the votes shall then be counted;

The person having the greatest number of votes for President, shall be the President, if such number be a majority of the whole number of Electors appointed; and if no person have such majority, then from the persons having the highest numbers not exceeding three on the list of those voted for as President, the House of Representatives shall choose immediately, by ballot, the President. But in choosing the President, the votes shall be taken by states, the representation from each state having one vote; a quorum for this purpose shall consist of a member or members from two-thirds of the states, and a majority of all the states shall be necessary to a choice. And if the House of Representatives shall not choose a President whenever the right of choice shall devolve upon them, before the fourth day of March next following, then the Vice-President shall act as President, as in case of the death or other constitutional disability of the President.

The person having the greatest number of votes as Vice-President, shall be the Vice-President, if such number be a majority of the whole number of Electors appointed, and if no person have a majority, then from the two highest numbers on the list, the Senate shall choose the Vice-President; a quorum for the purpose shall consist of two-thirds of the whole number of Senators, and a majority of the whole number shall be necessary to a choice. But no person constitutionally ineligible to the office of President shall be eligible to that of Vice-President of the United States.

Amendment XIII

Passed by Congress January 31, 1865. Ratified December 6, 1865. Note: A portion of Article IV, section 2, of the Constitution was superseded by the 13th amendment.

Section 1.

Neither slavery nor involuntary servitude, except as a punishment for crime whereof the party shall have been duly convicted, shall exist within the United States, or any place subject to their jurisdiction.

Section 2.

Congress shall have power to enforce this article by appropriate legislation.

Amendment XIV

Passed by Congress June 13, 1866. Ratified July 9, 1868. Note: Article I, section 2, of the Constitution was modified by section 2 of the 14th amendment.

Section 1.

All persons born or naturalized in the United States, and subject to the jurisdiction thereof, are citizens of the United States and of the State wherein they reside. No State shall make or enforce any law which shall abridge the privileges or immunities of citizens of the United States; nor shall any State deprive any person of life, liberty, or property, without due process of law; nor deny to any person within its jurisdiction the equal protection of the laws.

Section 2.

Representatives shall be apportioned among the several States according to their respective numbers, counting the whole number of persons in each State, excluding Indians not taxed. But when the right to vote at any election for the choice of electors for President and Vice-President of the United States, Representatives in Congress, the Executive and Judicial officers of a State, or the members of the Legislature thereof, is denied to any of the male inhabitants of such State, being twenty-one years of age, and citizens of the United States, or in any way abridged, except for participation in rebellion, or other crime, the basis of representation therein shall be reduced in the proportion which the number of such male citizens shall bear to the whole number of male citizens twenty-one years of age in such State.

Section 3.

No person shall be a Senator or Representative in Congress, or elector of President and Vice-President, or hold any office, civil or military, under the United States, or under any State, who, having previously taken an oath, as a member of Congress, or as an officer of the United States, or as a member of any State legislature, or as an executive or judicial officer of any State, to support the Constitution of the United States, shall have engaged in insurrection or rebellion against the same, or given aid or comfort to the enemies thereof. But Congress may by a vote of two-thirds of each House, remove such disability.

Section 4.

The validity of the public debt of the United States, authorized by law, including debts incurred for payment of pensions and bounties for services in suppressing insurrection or rebellion, shall not be questioned. But neither the United States nor any State shall assume or pay any debt or obligation incurred in aid of insurrection or rebellion against the United States, or any claim for the loss or emancipation of any slave; but all such debts, obligations and claims shall be held illegal and void.

Section 5.

The Congress shall have the power to enforce, by appropriate legislation, the provisions of this article.

Amendment XV

Passed by Congress February 26, 1869. Ratified February 3, 1870.

Section 1.

The right of citizens of the United States to vote shall not be denied or abridged by the United States or by any State on account of race, color, or previous condition of servitude.

Section 2.

The Congress shall have the power to enforce this article by appropriate legislation.

Amendment XVI

Passed by Congress July 2, 1909. Ratified February 3, 1913. Note: Article I, section 9, of the Constitution was modified by amendment 16.

The Congress shall have power to lay and collect taxes on incomes, from whatever source derived, without apportionment among the several States, and without regard to any census or enumeration.

Amendment XVII

Passed by Congress May 13, 1912. Ratified April 8, 1913. Note: Article I, section 3, of the Constitution was modified by the 17th amendment.

The Senate of the United States shall be composed of two Senators from each State, elected by the people thereof, for six years; and each Senator shall have one vote. The electors in each State shall have the qualifications requisite for electors of the most numerous branch of the State legislatures.

When vacancies happen in the representation of any State in the Senate, the executive authority of such State shall issue writs of election to fill such vacancies: Provided, That the legislature of any State may empower the executive thereof to make temporary appointments until the people fill the vacancies by election as the legislature may direct.

This amendment shall not be so construed as to affect the election or term of any Senator chosen before it becomes valid as part of the Constitution.

Amendment XVIII

Passed by Congress December 18, 1917. Ratified January 16, 1919. Repealed by amendment 21.

Section 1.

After one year from the ratification of this article the manufacture, sale, or transportation of intoxicating liquors within, the importation thereof into, or the exportation thereof from the United States and all territory subject to the jurisdiction thereof for beverage purposes is hereby prohibited.

Section 2.

The Congress and the several States shall have concurrent power to enforce this article by appropriate legislation.

Section 3.

This article shall be inoperative unless it shall have been ratified as an amendment to the Constitution by the legislatures of the several States, as provided in the Constitution, within seven years from the date of the submission hereof to the States by the Congress.

Amendment XIX

Passed by Congress June 4, 1919. Ratified August 18, 1920.

The right of citizens of the United States to vote shall not be denied or abridged by the United States or by any State on account of sex.

Congress shall have power to enforce this article by appropriate legislation.

Amendment XX

Passed by Congress March 2, 1932. Ratified January 23, 1933. Note: Article I, section 4, of the Constitution was modified by section 2 of this amendment. In addition, a portion of the 12th amendment was superseded by section 3.

Section 1.

The terms of the President and the Vice President shall end at noon on the 20th day of January, and the terms of Senators and Representatives at noon on the 3d day of January, of the years in which such terms would have ended if this article had not been ratified; and the terms of their successors shall then begin.

Section 2.

The Congress shall assemble at least once in every year, and such meeting shall begin at noon on the 3d day of January, unless they shall by law appoint a different day.

Section 3.

If, at the time fixed for the beginning of the term of the President, the President elect shall have died, the Vice President elect shall become President. If a President shall not have been chosen before the time fixed for the beginning of his term, or if the President elect shall have failed to qualify, then the Vice President elect shall act as President until a President shall have qualified; and the Congress may by law provide for the case wherein neither a President elect nor a Vice President elect shall have qualified, declaring who shall then act as President, or the manner in which one who is to act shall be selected, and such person shall act accordingly until a President or Vice President shall have qualified.

Section 4.

The Congress may by law provide for the case of the death of any of the persons from whom the House of Representatives may choose a President whenever the right of choice shall have devolved upon them, and for the case of the death of any of the persons from whom the Senate may choose a Vice President whenever the right of choice shall have devolved upon them.

Section 5.

Sections 1 and 2 shall take effect on the 15th day of October following the ratification of this article.

Section 6.

This article shall be inoperative unless it shall have been ratified as an amendment to the Constitution by the legislatures of three-fourths of the several States within seven years from the date of its submission.

Amendment XXI

Passed by Congress February 20, 1933. Ratified December 5, 1933.

Section 1.

The eighteenth article of amendment to the Constitution of the United States is hereby repealed.

Section 2.

The transportation or importation into any State, Territory, or possession of the United States for delivery or use therein of intoxicating liquors, in violation of the laws thereof, is hereby prohibited.

Section 3.

This article shall be inoperative unless it shall have been ratified as an amendment to the Constitution by conventions in the several States, as provided in the Constitution, within seven years from the date of the submission hereof to the States by the Congress.

Amendment XXII

Passed by Congress March 21, 1947. Ratified February 27, 1951.

Section 1.

No person shall be elected to the office of the President more than twice, and no person who has held the office of President, or acted as President, for more than two years of a term to which some other person was elected President shall be elected to the office of the President more than once. But this Article shall not apply to any person holding the office of President when this Article was proposed by the Congress, and shall not prevent any person who may be holding the office of President, or acting as President, during the term within which this Article becomes operative from holding the office of President or acting as President during the remainder of such term.

Section 2.

This article shall be inoperative unless it shall have been ratified as an amendment to the Constitution by the legislatures of three-fourths of the several States within seven years from the date of its submission to the States by the Congress.

Amendment XXIII

Passed by Congress June 16, 1960. Ratified March 29, 1961.

Section 1.

The District constituting the seat of Government of the United States shall appoint in such manner as the Congress may direct: A number of electors of President and Vice President equal to the whole number of Senators and Representatives in Congress to which the District would be entitled if it were a State, but in no event more than the least populous State; they shall be in addition to those appointed by the States, but they shall be considered, for the purposes of the election of President and Vice President, to be electors appointed by a State; and they shall meet in the District and perform such duties as provided by the twelfth article of amendment.

Section 2.

The Congress shall have power to enforce this article by appropriate legislation.

Amendment XXIV

Passed by Congress August 27, 1962. Ratified January 23, 1964.

Section 1.

The right of citizens of the United States to vote in any primary or other election for President or Vice President, for electors for President or Vice President, or for Senator or Representative in Congress, shall not be denied or abridged by the United States or any State by reason of failure to pay any poll tax or other tax.

Section 2.

The Congress shall have power to enforce this article by appropriate legislation.

Amendment XXV

Passed by Congress July 6, 1965. Ratified February 10, 1967. Note: Article II, section 1, of the Constitution was affected by the 25th amendment.

Section 1.

In case of the removal of the President from office or of his death or resignation, the Vice President shall become President.

Section 2.

Whenever there is a vacancy in the office of the Vice President, the President shall nominate a Vice President who shall take office upon confirmation by a majority vote of both Houses of Congress.

Section 3.

Whenever the President transmits to the President pro tempore of the Senate and the Speaker of the House of Representatives his written declaration that he is unable to discharge the powers and duties of his office, and until he transmits to them a written declaration to the contrary, such powers and duties shall be discharged by the Vice President as Acting President.

Section 4.

Whenever the Vice President and a majority of either the principal officers of the executive departments or of such other body as Congress may by law provide, transmit to the President pro tempore of the Senate and the Speaker of the House of Representatives their written declaration that the President is unable to discharge the powers and duties of his office, the Vice President shall immediately assume the powers and duties of the office as Acting President.

Thereafter, when the President transmits to the President pro tempore of the Senate and the Speaker of the House of Representatives his written declaration that no inability exists, he shall resume the powers and duties of his office unless the Vice President and a majority of either the principal officers of the executive department or of such other body as Congress may by law provide, transmit within four days to the President pro tempore of the Senate and the Speaker of the House of Representatives their written declaration that the President is unable to discharge the powers and duties of his office. Thereupon Congress shall decide the issue, assembling within forty-eight hours for that purpose if not in session. If the Congress, within twenty-one days after receipt of the latter written declaration, or, if Congress is not in session, within twenty-one days after Congress is required to assemble, determines by two-thirds vote of both Houses that the President is unable to discharge the powers and duties of his office, the Vice President shall continue to discharge the same as Acting President; otherwise, the President shall resume the powers and duties of his office.

Amendment XXVI

Passed by Congress March 23, 1971. Ratified July 1, 1971. Note: Amendment 14, section 2, of the Constitution was modified by section 1 of the 26th amendment.

Section 1.

The right of citizens of the United States, who are eighteen years of age or older, to vote shall not be denied or abridged by the United States or by any State on account of age.

Section 2.

The Congress shall have power to enforce this article by appropriate legislation.

Amendment XXVII

Originally proposed Sept. 25, 1789. Ratified May 7, 1992.

No law, varying the compensation for the services of the Senators and Representatives, shall take effect, until an election of Representatives shall have intervened.

Endnotes

1   Neal Boortz, *Somebody's Gotta Say It* (New York: HarperCollins, 2007), 172

2   Ibid., 309

3   Arthur C. Brooks, *The Road to Freedom* (New York: Basic Books, 2012), 6

4   Ibid., 57

5   Yuval Levin, *The Great Debate* (New York: Basic books, 2014), xii

6   Michelle Caruso-Cabrera, *You Know I'm Right* (New York: Threshold Editions, 2010), 1

7   Ben Carson, MD, *One Nation* (New York: Penguin Group, 2014), 14

8   Ibid., 16

9   Joe Scarborough, *The Right Path* (New York: Random House, 2013), 49

10 Johnathan Gentry, *YouTube* (August 14 and 15, 2014)

11 Thomas Sowell, *Wealth, Poverty and Politics* (New York: Basic Books, 2015), 75

12 Heather Mac Donald, "The Danger of the 'Black Lives Matter' Movement," *Imprimis*, Volume 45, Number 4 (2016): 2

13 Ibid., 2,3,5

14 Ibid., 5

15 M. Night Shyamalan, *I Got Schooled* (New York: Simon & Schuster, 2013), 15

16 Caruso-Cabrera, *You Know I'm Right*, 122

17 Ibid., 116

18 Shyamalan, *I Got Schooled*, 79-103

19 Ibid., 107-133

20 Ibid., 158, 164

21 Ibid., 164-182, 234

22 Ibid., 200-207

23 Larry P. Arnn, *The Founders' Key* (Nashville: Thomas Nelson, 2012), 87

24 Ibid., 19

25 Ibid., 71

26 Ibid., 74

27 Mike Patton, "Who Owns the Most U.S. Debt?", *Forbes*, October 28, 2014, http://www.forbes.com/sites/mikepatton/2014/10/28

28 Krugman, Paul, "Nobody Understands Debt," *The New York Times*, January 1, 2012, New York edition, Opinion Pages

29 Brooks Jackson, "Who Holds Our Debt?", *Factcheck*, November 19, 2013, http://www.factcheck.org/2013/11

30 Barack Obama, *Congressional Record—Senate*, March 16, 2006, S2237-S2238

31 Department of the Treasury, Bureau of Fiscal Service, *Final Monthly*

Treasury Statement for Fiscal Year 2015 Through September 30, 2015 (October 2015)

32 Congressional Budget Office, *The Federal Budget In 2015* (January 2016)

33 Ibid.

34 Department of the Treasury, Bureau of Fiscal Service, *Final Monthly Treasury Statement for Fiscal Year 2015 Through September 30, 2015* (October, 2015)

35 Congressional Budget Office, *The 2016 Long-Term Budget Outlook* (July 2016), 9

36 George Washington, "Farewell Address," September 19, 1796

37 Sowell, *Wealth, Poverty and Politics*, 1

38 Ibid., 52

39 Ibid., 57

40 Ibid., 70-71

41 Ibid., 93, 98

42 Ibid., 98

43 Ibid., 98-99

44 Ibid., 114-115

45 Ibid., 115

46 Ibid., 148

47 Cohn, Emily, "Here's How Much You Have to Earn To Be In The 1 Percent In Each State," *Huffington Post*, January 26, 2015, http://www.huffingtonpost.com/2015/01/26

48 Joseph E. Stiglitz, *The Price of Inequality* (New York: W.W. Norton & Company, Inc., 2012), xvii

49 Ibid., 3

50 Sowell, *Wealth, Poverty and Politics*, 235

51 Ibid., 168

52 Ibid., 177-190

53 Jeffrey Dorfman, "Almost Everything You Have Been Told About the Minimum Wage Is False," *Forbes,* January 30, 2014, http://www.forbes.com/sites/jeffreydorfman/2014/01/30

54 Ibid

55 Ibid

56 Ibid

57 Mathew Spalding, "Thomas Jefferson Still Lives," *Heritage.org.* Heritage Foundation, February 25, 2001 http://s3.amazonaws.com/thf_media/2001/pdf/em724.pdf

58 "Over-regulated America," *The Economist*, February 18th—24th 2012, 9

59 Caruso-Cabrera, *You Know I'm Right*, 205

60 "Over-regulated America," 9

61 Ibid., 9

62 Ibid., 9

63 Ibid., 9

64 Greg Orman, *A Declaration of Independents* (Austin: Greenleaf Book

Group Press, 2016), 253

65 Karl Marx and Frederick Engels, *The Communist Manifesto* (New York: International Publishers Co., Inc., 1948), 30

66 David M. Walker, *Comeback America* (New York: Random House, 2010), 63-64

67 Ibid., 64

68 Michael D. Tanner, "Medicare and Social Security Tabs Coming Due," *Reason*, March 2015

69 Walker, *Comeback America*, 70

70 Ibid., 71

71 Ibid., 71

72 Caruso-Cabrera, *You Know I'm Right*, 75

73 Alex Nowrasteh, "Immigration Reform Ideas for the New Speaker," *The Hill*, October 30, 2015, http://thehill.com/blogs/pundits-blog/immigration/258634-immigration-reform-ideas-for-the-new-speaker

74 Lee Edwards, "What this Washington Post Columnist Got Wrong in Analysis of Conservatives," *The Daily Signal*, February 24, 2016, http://dailysignal.com/2016/02/24

75 Boortz, *Somebody's Gotta Say It*, 101

76 Ibid., 102

77 Ibid., 51-52

78 Caruso-Cabrera, *You Know I'm Right*, 50

79 Ibid., 50

80 Katherine Q. Seelye, "Massachusetts Chief's Tack in Drug War: Steer Addicts to Rehab, Not Jail," *The New York Times*, January 24, 2016, http://www.nytimes.com/2016/01/25

81 Ibid

82 Jill Pohl, "Treatment, Not Prison, May Be the Problem Solution To America's Drug Problem," *Elite Daily*, May 15, 2015

83 Ibid

84 Orman, *A Declaration of Independents*, 87

85 Sowell, *Wealth, Poverty and Politics*, 197

86 Michelle Fox, "Billionaire Ken Langone: The grim reaper is not far away," CNBC, November 8, 2016, http://www.cnbc.com/2016/11/08/billionaire-ken-langone-the-grim-reaper-is-not-far-away.html

87 Scarborough, *The Right Path*, 61

88 Brooks, *The Road to Freedom*, 131

89 Orman, *A Declaration of Independents*, 49

Acknowledgements

There are several people I would like to credit and thank for giving me the inspiration to bring my thoughts to print, including two I haven't spoken with in close to 40 years. Professor John Jolley, who made history come alive for me while I was studying finance and accounting at Bryant. Jerry Ramos, my direct supervisor when I was a resident assistant at Bryant, who believed that I would do more in my life than work in financial services, and whose words I have always remembered. Anna Scala, a friend who for many years has encouraged me to go public with my thoughts. William Woods and his family for their friendship, love and spirited conversation. My parents, for their love and introducing me to their friends who spanned different races, religions, and sexual orientations. My son, Ryan, because when I am gone I want him to always remember what his dad stood for, and I hope I inspire him to do what he can to make this a kinder, more fiscally sound world.

Most importantly, I want to thank the girl of my dreams, my best friend and wife, Stephanie. She is beautiful inside and out, smart, and makes me laugh. She has amazingly put up with me for over thirty-one years, and I am so thankful. Without her love, patience and encouragement, I would not have been able to take the time to do the necessary research and put my thoughts in writing.

About the Author

David A. Ellison is a partner with his wife, Stephanie, in the Ellison Homes Team, a RE/MAX affiliate. He received his B.S. from Bryant College (now Bryant University), and is a Certified Financial Planner. He has been the editor and publisher of his own financial newsletter, and is very interested in history and politics. David and Stephanie live in Milford, CT, and have one child.

CPSIA information can be obtained
at www.ICGtesting.com
Printed in the USA
FFOW03n1606110417
34316FF